Essential Non-fiction
Teaching & Planning Guide

Contents

Welcome to Literacy World!

Literacy World is a complete fiction and non-fiction literacy programme for juniors. It offers resources for shared and independent work for both reading and writing. The fiction and non-fiction strands both work in the same way, and can be used alongside each other.

In this updated edition, we have brought *Literacy World* into line with the latest advice on whole-class teaching, flexible planning and child-friendly target setting. The one-, two- and three-week units of work reflect the National Literacy Strategy's Medium Term Plans. As ever, the starting point for the programme has been to maintain a selection of superb quality texts for both fiction and non-fiction.

Shared Reading and Writing Components

FICTION for each of Years 3–6 (Primary 4–Primary 7)

FICTION TEACHING & PLANNING GUIDE

ESSENTIAL FICTION ANTHOLOGY

FICTION SKILLS BIG BOOK

WHOLE CLASS INTERACTIVE SOFTWARE

NON-FICTION for each of Years 3–6 (Primary 4–Primary 7)

NON-FICTION TEACHING & PLANNING GUIDE

ESSENTIAL NON-FICTION ANTHOLOGY

NON-FICTION SKILLS BIG BOOK

WHOLE CLASS INTERACTIVE SOFTWARE

Literacy World also provides an extensive range of guided reading books and teaching support for both fiction and non-fiction, for children of all reading ability. For further information on the Literacy World Guided Reading components, please see the inside back cover.

Using Literacy World in the Classroom

Planning

Literacy World provides complete units of work for both fiction and non-fiction, in a flexible way that reflects the genre requirements and teaching objectives of the term. Across the fiction and non-fiction strands, *Literacy World* provides 14 weeks of work for Term 1, 11 for Term 2 and 11 for Term 3. These are broken down in the following way:

STAGE/TERM	FICTION	NON-FICTION
Stage 1 Term 1	5 units over 9 weeks	2 units over 5 weeks
Stage 1 Term 2	3 units over 7 weeks	2 units over 4 weeks
Stage 1 Term 3	5 units over 8 weeks	2 units over 3 weeks

The units of work vary in length, from one week to three weeks. Some of the sessions are optional, putting the teacher in control of how much time he or she wants to spend on a particular focus. For example, in Stage 1 Non-fiction, Unit 2 on note-making and dictionaries is a flexible one- or two-week unit. The optional sessions provide consolidation and reinforcement of the key teaching points covered in Week 1.

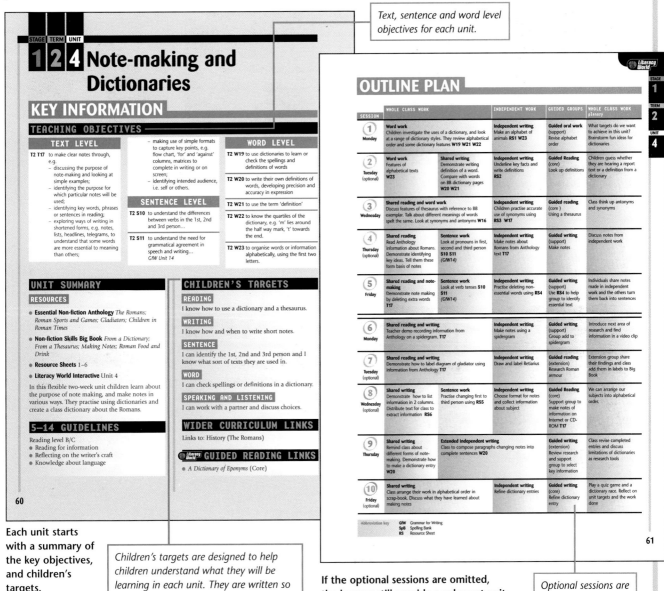

Text, sentence and word level objectives for each unit.

Each unit starts with a summary of the key objectives, and children's targets.

Children's targets are designed to help children understand what they will be learning in each unit. They are written so that children can be involved in self-assessment and can understand what is required to make progress.

If the optional sessions are omitted, the lessons still provide a coherent unit of work of either one or two weeks.

Optional sessions are highlighted in grey.

SESSION ②

FOCUS

- **Can you identify and use further features of a non-chronological report?**

RESOURCES

- Essential Non-fiction Anthology pages 12–13 *About Elephants*
- Resource Sheet 2 *Comparing Elephants*
- Non-chronological reports on other animals

SHARED READING

Read Anthology pp 12–13.

◁⟩ **Listening focus** What additional information can we learn about elephants from this text?

Draw attention to the further features of this text not seen in the Big Book version. Talk about the purpose of headings, side headings, illustrations, diagrams, maps, and discuss reading strategies (e.g. starting with the heading, then scanning the whole page and returning to the main text before looking in detail at the illustrations).

Ask the children what they have found out about different types of elephant. Draw two columns on the board headed *African Elephant* and *Asian Elephant*. Ask the children to think about the different features of the elephant's appearance that you can compare, and enter them as headings for each row (e.g. *ears, trunks, foreheads, tusks*). Ask the children to supply information for each column. Explain a chart is the best way to compare information. *(Links with GfW, Unit 9)*

WORD WORK

Identify specific vocabulary in the shared text. Explain that non-fiction texts often include specialised technical vocabulary relating to a particular subject. Discuss strategies for reading and understanding the words in context and make a note of key words (e.g. *herbivores, Africa, mammals, habitat, trunk, matriarch*). Discuss the spelling as you write.

INDEPENDENT WRITING

Read through each statement on pages 12–13 in the Anthology and decide whether it is true or false for each type of elephant. Record findings on RS2.

GUIDED WRITING ⸺ EXTENSION

Using a non-chronological report on other animals (such as pets or wild animals) ask the children to help you devise a chart to show key differences. Discuss what information to include on the chart, and whether presenting information in a chart makes it easier to read.

PLENARY

Have a quiz on elephant facts, based on the children's independent work. Read out some of the statements and ask children to identify whether they are about African or Asian elephants.

SESSION ③

FOCUS

- **How do you organise information in a non-chronological report?**

RESOURCES

- Non-fiction Skills Big Book pages 14–15 *Writing Frame for Animal Report*
- Essential Non-fiction Anthology pages 12–13 *About Elephants*; pages 14–15 *Key Facts About Hippos*
- Resource Sheet 3 *Hippo Factsheet*
- Resource Sheet 4 *Hippo Report*

SENTENCE WORK

Write the word *hippo* on the board. Brainstorm with the class some information they know about hippos and note any key words and phrases. Encourage them to compose questions if they are not sure about the facts (e.g. *Do they eat other animals or just plants?*)

Read the statements about hippos (RS3, cut into strips) and give them out to pairs of children. Explain the information can be arranged into a non-chronological report with a paragraph for each category of information. Write the following headings on the board, one above the other but with space between: *Habitat, Appearance, Food*. Ask each pair to come out in turn and place their sentence under the correct heading. *(Links with GfW Unit 9.)* ⸺

SHARED WRITING

Planning for writing Look at Anthology pp.14–15 and explain that this gives detailed facts about hippos, but that it is not sorted in any way. Explain that you are going to use these facts to write a non-chronological report about hippos. Demonstrate how to read part of the text, identify a key fact and note it under a heading (habitat, appearance or food).

Introduce the writing frame (Big Book pp.14–15) and point out that the headings are similar to those used for *About Elephants* (Anthology pp.12–13). Reread the first paragraph about the elephant and remind children that this is an opening definition that introduces the subject. Point out that the information under each sub-heading corresponds to a paragraph.

Demonstration writing Model composing an opening definition for the first paragraph. It should include specific or technical vocabulary, an impersonal style with generalised participants and use the present tense. (See RS4 'Hippo Report' for exemplar shared writing text). Keep this work to use in Session 4.

INDEPENDENT READING

Remind the children that non-fiction texts answer questions. Recap some useful question words (e.g. *What? Where? When? Why? How?*) Tell them to draw a Question Hand and label the fingers. Ask the children to read through all the information on Anthology pp.14–15 about hippos, and write one question about it for each question word.

Speaking and listening

*Planned opportunities for developing speaking and listening skills are provided. There are specific activities under the headings **Time out for discussion, Time out for thinking** and **Listening focus**.*

Guided writing

Support for guided writing sessions follows on from the shared work. These are often differentiated for ability groups.

Grammar for Writing/ Spelling Bank

*Where appropriate, references are given to units in **Grammar for Writing** and **Spelling Bank** activities. However, access to these documents is not obligatory in order to run the **Literacy World** sessions. The references are there if further work on the focus is required.*

SHARED READING

? Limbering up Think of three questions about snakes to answer. Take feedback and note some of the most interesting or original questions.

Introduce the idea of writing a report on snakes for a class book on animals. Explain that you will need some source material with facts about snakes. Turn to pp16–17 in the Big Book. Can they remember what this type of chart is called? *(spidergram)*. Begin to read through, drawing attention to the way the information is presented and contrasting this with a report (e.g. *bullet points and notes rather than complete sentences arranged in paragraphs*).

Involve the children in identifying specific facts, making use of the features of the spidergram.

Talk about using this information in a report – challenge the children to compose complete sentences orally using some of the facts from the spidergram.

INDEPENDENT READING

Children read another source of information about snakes and continue to make notes, categorising the information in the same way as on the spidergram.

GUIDED READING   EXTENSION

Use an ICT source to research further information about snakes, e.g. a CD-ROM encyclopedia. Point out features that help you with this type of text *(video clips, links to other subjects, sound, etc.)*

PLENARY

Take feedback from the independent task and add further notes to the spidergram. Keep it for Session 8.

SESSION 8

FOCUS

- **How do you turn notes into a non-chronological report?**

RESOURCES

- Non-fiction Skills Big Book pages 14–15 *Writing Frame for Animal Report;* pages 16–17 *Snakes*

SHARED WRITING AND SENTENCE WORK

Refer back to the information on the spidergram. Tell the children that you are going to turn the notes into a non-chronological report for the class book on animals.

Demonstration writing Using the non-chronological writing frame in Big Book pp.14–15, demonstrate writing the information for two sub-headings *(opening definition* and *habitat)* paying particular attention to the language features of reports. Draw attention to the way that each sentence in the paragraph relates to the heading. Refer to the notes and involve the children in composing sentences that use specific words from the spidergram.

34

Ready, steady, write Invite the children to work in pairs to transform the data on the spidergram into a 3rd paragraph about what snakes eat. Ask two children to have their work ready to discuss in the plenary.

INDEPENDENT WRITING

Remind the children that information can also be presented in a labelled diagram. Draw a simple diagram of a snake on the board for the children to copy. Ask them to label the skin, ears, eyes, fangs and poison using the information on the spidergram. Keep these diagrams for use in Session 10.

GUIDED WRITING   SUPPORT

Work with the group to help them extract the information from the spidergram to complete the labels for their snakes.

PLENARY

Share the work completed by the two children. Examine how language is used differently in report texts, spidergrams and labelled illustrations. Which information is the easiest to read? Which is the most interesting?

SESSION 9

FOCUS

- **Can you use the features of a report in your own writing?**

RESOURCES

- Non-fiction Skills Big Book pages 16–17 *Snakes*
- Essential Non-fiction Anthology pages 18–19 *Snakes*

SENTENCE WORK

Time out for discussion Ask the children to turn to a partner and to think of two things they know about nouns *(naming words, come after 'the' or 'a')*.

Take in their ideas and draw attention to the difference between common nouns and proper nouns. Brainstorm a list of animals found in a zoo. Write the names on the board and discuss placing the commas to separate the nouns in a list. Tell them to omit the comma after 'and' at the end of a list.

SHARED READING

Review the information that has already been included in the report on snakes: opening definition, habitat, food and appearance (labelled diagram) and start to collect additional information for the remaining paragraphs.

Read through Anthology, pages 18–19. Ask the children to pick out the information on 'breeding', 'killing prey' and 'interesting facts' . Demonstrate how to make notes and add to the spidergram (e.g. by attaching post-it notes to the Big Book page).

Guided reading

Suggestions are given for reinforcing the focus of the shared and independent work in guided reading sessions, using any suitable book. Links to books from **Literacy World** *Guided Readers are given in the Key Information.*

Shared reading and writing

Reading and writing are covered equally. Where the focus is on demonstration writing, exemplar texts are provided for support.

Independent work

Suggestions follow on from the shared reading and writing. Where appropriate, these are differentiated for lower ability groups (support) and higher ability groups (extension). The activities take a range of forms, including group discussions, ICT and research, sometimes making use of photocopiable Resource Sheets.

Recurring activities

There are a number of activities that occur regularly throughout the programme, which provide opportunities for active participation.

?	✏	〰	🗨	💭	🔊
Limbering up Warm-up oral games, puzzles and questions, linked to the focus of the unit.	**Ready, steady, write** Children write on individual whiteboards.	**Living sentences** Physically constructing and deconstructing sentences.	**Time out for discussion** Giving children, in pairs, brief discussion time during whole class work.	**Time out for thinking** Giving children brief thinking time during whole class work.	**Listening focus** Giving children a specific question or focus while the teacher reads. Feedback is generally required.

Literacy World Interactive) How to use Literacy World Interactive

Literacy World Interactive CD-ROMs add a new dimension to whole-class sessions, providing resources to help the teacher integrate ICT into literacy in a meaningful way as they are linked directly to the units of work in the *Teaching and Planning Guide*. For each stage of *Literacy World* there is one CD for fiction and one CD for non-fiction.

On each of the CDs there are:

- electronic versions of the Big Book pages
- additional stimulus material, in the form of audio recordings, short video clips and photographs
- a range of interactive word and sentence activities
- some additional reading extracts
- Resource Sheets for independent work edit and customise
- notes to help the teacher make the most of the resources

The activities in *Literacy World Interactive* can be used alongside the activities suggested in the units of work in this Teaching and Planning Guide. They are intended as an optional way of extending literacy teaching in a fun and motivating environment, and can be used to reinforce and consolidate learning.

Details of the resources for each of the *Literacy World* units of work are given at the end of teaching notes for that unit. Notes on how to use the interactive resources are on the CD itself.

Literacy World and the NLS Objectives

Literacy World covers the full range of NLS Objectives, as described in the NLS *Framework for Teaching*, and mirrors the approach set out in the Medium Term Plans. These charts show how the objectives have been linked together to form units of work.

STAGE 1 TERM 1

	UNIT TITLE/FOCUS	WEEKS	LITERACY WORLD RESOURCES		TEXT		SENTENCE		WORD	SPEAKING & LISTENING	OUTCOME
1	Comparing Fact and Fiction	2	Essential Non-fiction Anthology: *About Skateboarding; Pride Comes Before a Fall; Alton Towers map* Non-fiction Skills Big Book: *Features; First Day; Victorian Schools; Over the Phone; World of Adventures*	T17	understand the distinction between fact and fiction	S1	to use grammar to decipher new or unfamiliar words	W8	how the spelling of verbs alters when 'ing' is added	Collaborative talk to generate ideas	Evaluation of non-fiction texts
				T18	notice differences between the style and structure of fiction and non-fiction writing	S9	notice and investigate a range of other devices for presenting text	W14	to infer the meaning of unknown words from context	Using language of non-fiction	
				T19	to locate information using contents, index etc.	S10	identify the boundaries between separate sentences	W15	to secure understanding of the purpose and organisation of the dictionary		
				T21	read information passages and identify main points			W16	understand the purpose and organisation of the thesaurus		
				T22	to make a simple record of information from texts read						
2	Non-chronological Reports	2	Essential Non-fiction Anthology: *About Elephants; Key Facts About Hippos; Mighty Mammals; Snake spidergram; Crocodiles* Non-fiction Skills Big Book: *What are Report Texts?; About Elephants; Writing frame; Spidergram for Snakes; Crocodiles*	T19	locate information, using contents, index, headings, sub-headings, page nos., bibliographies	S9	notice and investigate a range of other devices for presenting text	W5	identify misspelt words in own writing; keep spelling logs; learn to spell them	Discussing ways to present information	Written report Notes
				T20	compare the way information is presented e.g. comparing a variety of information texts including IT-based sources	S13	use commas to separate items in a list	W13	to collect new words from reading		
				T21	read information passages, and identify main points or gist of text, e.g. by noting or underlining key words or phrases, listing the 4 or 5 main points covered			W14	to infer the meaning of unknown words from context		
				T23	write simple non-chronological reports from known information, using notes made to organise and present ideas; write for a known audience						

7

STAGE 1 TERM 2

	UNIT TITLE/FOCUS	WEEKS	LITERACY WORLD RESOURCES	TEXT	SENTENCE	WORD	SPEAKING & LISTENING	OUTCOME
3	Instructions	2	Essential Non-fiction Anthology: *How to Make a Twizzer; How to Make a Balancing Bird; How to Play Tiddly-winks* Non-fiction Skills Big Book: *The Magic Wood; How to Get to the Museum; Funny Face Biscuits; Beautiful Bathing*	T12 identify the specific purposes of instructional texts T13 discuss the merits and limitations of particular instructional texts T14 understand how written instructions are organised T15 read and follow simple instructions T16 write instructions	S9 experiment with deleting words in sentences to see which are essential to retain meaning and which are not S10 understand the differences between verbs in the first, second and third person S11 understand the need for grammatical agreement in speech and writing	W4 discriminate syllables in reading and spelling W6 to use independent spelling strategies W7 to practise new spellings regularly by Look, Say, Cover, Write Check	Listening to and following oral instructions	Following instructions Written instructions
4	Note-making and Dictionaries	2	Essential Non-fiction Anthology: *The Romans; Roman Sports and Games; Gladiators; Children in Roman Times* Non-fiction Skills Big Book: *From a Dictionary; From a Thesaurus; Making Notes; Roman Food and Drink*	T17 to make clear notes through, e.g. – discussing the purpose of note-making and looking at simple examples; – identifying the purpose for which particular notes will be used; – identifying key words in reading – exploring ways of writing in shortened forms, e.g. notes, lists, headlines, telegrams, to understand that some words are more essential to meaning than others; – making use of simple formats to capture key points, e.g. flow chart, 'for' and 'against' columns, matrices to complete in writing or on screen; – identifying intended audience	S10 understand the differences between verbs in the 1st, 2nd and 3rd person S11 understand the need for grammatical agreement in speech and writing	W19 use dictionaries to learn or check the spellings and definitions W20 write their own definitions of words W21 use the term 'definition' W22 know the quartiles of the dictionary W23 organise words or information alphabetically, using the first two letters.	Summarising information	Class dictionary

STAGE 1 TERM 3

UNIT TITLE/FOCUS	WEEKS	LITERACY WORLD RESOURCES	TEXT	SENTENCE	WORD	SPEAKING & LISTENING	OUTCOME
5 Writing letters/letters for different purposes	2	Essential Non-fiction Anthology: *Recount; Complaint; Explanation; Congratulation; Uplands Farm Brochure; Kinds of Letters* Non-fiction Skills Big Book: *Sending Messages; Letter of Enquiry; Formal Letter* with writing frames	T16 read examples of letters written for a range of purposes T19 summarize orally in one sentence the content of a text and the main point it is making T20 write letters, notes and messages linked to work in other subjects T21 use IT to bring to a published form T22 experiment with recounting the same event in a variety of ways T23 organise letters into simple paragraphs T26 summarise in writing the content of a passage or text and the main point it is making	S1 use awareness of grammar to decipher new or unfamiliar words S3 ensure grammatical agreement in speech and writing of pronouns and verbs S6 investigate through reading and writing how words and phrases can signal time sequences	W1 revise the spelling of words containing each of the long vowel phonemes W6 use independent spelling strategies W7 practise new spellings regularly by 'look, say, cover, write, check'	Using informal and formal language appropriately	Range of letters for different purposes and audiences
6 Alphabetical texts	2	Essential Non-fiction Anthology: *Hobbies; Sea Fishing; Seamount Junior Fishing Club* Non-fiction Skills Big Book: *Yellow Pages; Hobbies Dictionary; Swimming; Directory Checklist; Writing Frame*	T17 scan indexes, directories and IT sources etc., to locate information quickly and accurately T18 locate books by classification in class or school libraries T21 use IT to bring to a published form – discuss relevance of layout, font, etc. to audience T24 make alphabetically ordered texts – use information from other subjects, own experience or derived from other information books T26 to summarise in writing the content of a passage or text and the main point it is making.	S7 become aware of the use of commas in marking grammatical boundaries within sentences	W3 read and spell correctly high-frequency words W14 to explore homonyms W15 understand that some dictionaries provide further information about words which can provide a guide to spelling		Class encyclopedia

Literacy World and the Scottish 5–14 Guidelines

Literacy World has been developed with many aspects of the 5–14 Guidelines in mind, and teachers will find it works well in the Scottish classroom.

- Stage 1 is suitable for Primary 4
- Stage 2 is suitable for Primary 5
- Stage 3 is suitable for Primary 6
- Stage 4 is suitable for Primary 7

5–14 Reading and Writing Strands

In general, *Literacy World* Stages 1 and 2 are suitable for children working at Levels B and C of the Attainment Targets. Stages 3 and 4 are suitable for children working approximately at Levels C and D. At the start of the teaching notes for each unit, you will find detailed reading levels for that unit, along with a summary of how the resources and teaching suggestions match the Programme of Study for reading.

Opportunities to develop writing skills are interwoven throughout the units, and *Literacy World* recognises the importance of writing by dedicating approximately half of the sessions to different forms of writing. Children are led through the supportive structure of talking and planning for writing in response to their reading, teacher demonstration and scribing, and supported composition, before moving on to writing independently.

Literacy World offers opportunities for functional writing, personal writing and imaginative writing in a number of ways. The unit notes provide ideas for shared writing, independent writing using response journals and writing frames. Punctuation and structure, and knowledge about language are introduced in the shared reading and taught explicitly during shared writing. Many of the Resource Sheets give practice in the use of these skills.

Listening and Talking

Throughout *Literacy World*, there are planned opportunities for children to develop their communication skills, through discussing ideas and opinions in pairs and groups, giving feedback to the class, role-play and drama. These activities are highlighted in the notes under the headings **time out for discussion**, **time out for thinking**, **listening focus** and **role-play** as well as being built into the plenary sessions.

Literacy World and the Northern Ireland Curriculum

Literacy World supports reading, writing and talking and listening strands within the Programme of Study for English at Key Stage 2. *Literacy World* Stages 1 and 2 are suitable for children working at approximately Levels 2 and 3 of the Attainment Targets. Stages 3 and 4 are suitable for children working at approximately Levels 3 to 5.

Reading

Literacy World provides a full range of genres and text types, including narrative, poetry, playscripts and non-fiction. For a detailed description of these, please see the charts on page 7 to 9. The programme's approach encourages silent reading, reading for enjoyment and reading aloud for different audiences.

Children are given a range of reading activities including: listening to and understanding a range of texts; participating in shared reading; exploring stories and texts through discussion; expressing opinion and justifying responses; considering aspects of stories and the writer's craft.

Writing

Opportunities to develop writing skills are interwoven throughout the units, and *Literacy World* recognises the importance of writing by dedicating approximately half of the sessions to different forms of writing. Work on grammar and punctuation is built into writing. Children are led through the supportive structure of talking and planning for writing in response to their reading, teacher demonstration and scribing, and supported composition before moving on to writing independently.

The *Literacy World* fiction strand offers opportunities to write stories, diaries, poems, notes, dialogue and playscripts. The non-fiction strand gives support in writing reports, instructions, notes, explanations and discussions.

Talking and Listening

Throughout *Literacy World*, there are planned opportunities for children to develop their communication skills, through discussing ideas and opinions in pairs and groups, giving feedback to the class, role-play and drama. These activities are highlighted in the notes under the headings **time out for discussion**, **time out for thinking**, **listening focus** and **role-play** as well as being built into the plenary sessions.

1 1 1 Fact and Fiction

KEY INFORMATION

TEACHING OBJECTIVES

TEXT LEVEL

T1 T17 to understand the distinction between fact and fiction

T1 T18 to notice differences between the style and structure of fiction and non-fiction writing

T1 T19 to locate information using contents, index, etc.

T1 T21 to read information passages and identify main points

T1 T22 to make a simple record of information from texts read

SENTENCE LEVEL

T1 S1 to use grammar to decipher new or unfamiliar words

T1 S9 to notice and investigate a range of other devices for presenting text

T1 S10 to identify the boundaries between separate sentences

WORD LEVEL

T1 W8 to identify how the spelling of verbs alter when 'ing' is added

T1 W14 to infer the meaning of unknown words from context

T1 W15 to secure understanding of the purpose and organisation of the dictionary

T1 W16 to understand the purpose and organisation of the thesaurus

UNIT SUMMARY

RESOURCES

- **Essential Non-fiction Anthology** *About Skateboarding; Pride Comes Before a Fall; Alton Towers; Alton Towers map*
- **Non-fiction Skills Big Book** *Features; First Day; Victorian Schools; Over the Phone; World of Adventures*
- **Resource Sheets** 1–8
- **Literacy World Interactive** Unit 1

In this two-week unit children read and compare a range of fiction and non-fiction texts. They learn to identify and use the structure and language features of non-fiction. They present information in a range of different ways and finally write their own information leaflet using what they have learnt.

5–14 GUIDELINES

Reading level B/C
- Reading for information
- Awareness of genre
- Reflecting on the writer's craft

CHILDREN'S TARGETS

READING

I know the difference between fiction and non-fiction.

WRITING

I can write a leaflet and make it look interesting.

WORD

I know how to add 'ing' to verbs and how to use a thesaurus.

SPEAKING AND LISTENING

I can work with others to suggest ideas for writing.

WIDER CURRICULUM LINKS

The work on leaflets could be linked to ICT, combining text and graphics.

Literacy World GUIDED READING LINKS

- *The Search for Tutankhamen* (Core and Satellites)

OUTLINE PLAN

SESSION	WHOLE CLASS WORK		INDEPENDENT WORK	GUIDED GROUPS	WHOLE CLASS WORK plenary
1 Monday	**Shared reading** Distinguish between fiction and non- fiction books. Start list of features for each **T17 W15 W16**	**Sentence work** Devise questions to be answered from the text	**Independent reading** Sorting fact and fiction – Sort books into fiction and non-fiction and justify the decisions **T17**	**Guided reading** (support) Select non-fiction books and check features against class list	**Introduce Targets** What will you aim to do in this unit? What are the typical features of fiction and non-fiction?
2 Tuesday	**Shared reading** Discuss purpose of contents, index, glossary in the Anthology using **RS1 T19**	**Asking and answering questions** Draw question hand. Devise questions **S6**	**Independent reading** Extend sentences to give more information **S10**	**Guided reading** (core) Devise questions that can be answered from the text	Play 20 questions. Can you think of effective questions?
3 Wednesday	**Spelling** What happens when we add '-ing' to verbs **W8**	**Shared reading** Compare BB texts on Victorian schools and decide if fiction or non-fiction **T18**	**Independent reading** Fiction or non-fiction? – Sort sentences into fiction and non-fiction, using **RS2 T18**	**Guided reading** (extension) Look at links between fiction and non-fiction	Share independent work Play 'In the Dock' – justifying claims that sentences are fiction or non-fiction
4 Thursday	**Shared reading** Compare fiction and non-fiction texts on skateboarding in the Anthology and discuss the kinds of information they impart **T18**		**Independent reading** Creating titles – Invent 5 pairs of complementary titles for fiction and non-fiction books **T17**	**Guided reading** (support) Read and discuss non-fiction features	Are you clear about the contrasting features of fiction and non-fiction?
5 Friday	**Shared writing** Teacher scribing (use **RS3**). Turn notes into sentences. Discuss sentence boundaries **S10**		**Independent reading** Practise using the Anthology contents and index **RS4**	**Guided reading** (core) Look at different contents and indexes	We understand the uses of contents pages and indexes
6 Monday	**Sentence work** Explain purpose of graphic features of texts **S9** (GfW5)	**Shared reading** Read BB *Over the Phone* highlighting factual information	**Independent writing** Evaluate recount on **RS5**	**Guided writing** (extension) Sort information on **RS5**	Give oral account of a trip – class make notes on white boards
7 Tuesday	**Shared reading** Note key facts in brochure from Alton Towers (Anthology) on a spidergram **T21 T22**	**Sentence work** Discuss purpose of presenting texts in various ways **S9** (GfW5)	**Independent writing** Present information using different graphic devices **RS6**	**Guided reading** (support) Find examples of features of brochures	How many questions can we answer from the spidergram?
8 Wednesday	**Shared reading and writing** Demo, using Alton Towers in the Anthology, how to read charts, maps diagrams, etc. Present information in chart form **S9**	**Word work** Find base word from verbs ending in '-ing' **W8**	**Independent writing** Play the adding '-ing' game on **RS7**	**Guided writing** (core) Review presentation and devise questions	Discuss results of independent work on adding '-ing'
9 Thursday	**Word work** Investigate alphabetical order using a thesaurus **W16** **Shared writing** Scribe a class description of a theme park ride.	**Extended independent writing** Write the centre page of a brochure on a theme park **T22**		**Guided writing** (support) Select one ride to write about	Share entries from independent work and present them effectively
10 Friday	**Word work** Look up synonyms using a thesaurus. Talk about its purpose and organisation **W16**	**Shared reading** Introduce and discuss children's reading preferences using **RS8**	**Independent reading** Complete **RS8** and discuss reading preferences	**Guided writing** (support) Discuss relative merits of fiction or non-fiction	Have we achieved our targets for this unit?

TEACHING NOTES

SESSION (1)

FOCUS

- **What is the difference between fiction and non-fiction?**

RESOURCES

- Selection of fiction and non-fiction books, including dictionary and thesaurus
- Non-fiction Skills Big Book pages 2–3 *Features*

SHARED READING

Limbering up Ask the children whether they prefer to read fiction or non-fiction and take a class vote.

Introduce the unit by telling the children that they will be finding out about the difference between fiction and non-fiction and then writing a non-fiction text.

Ask the class to help you to sort a selection of books into two piles: fiction and non-fiction. Hold up each book in turn and ask the children which they think it is, then look through the pages for evidence.

Use the chart on pages 2–3 of the Big Book to start a class checklist of the features for each genre (e.g. *title, contents or chapters, glossary, photographs or illustrations, formal/informal language*).

Check that the children know the difference between a dictionary and a thesaurus. Talk about the structure and organisation of a dictionary and demonstrate how to use it.

SENTENCE WORK

Explain to the class that non-fiction books answer questions the reader may have about a topic. Look again at the non-fiction books sorted earlier. What questions might each text answer?

Hold up one of the non-fiction books and brainstorm questions that might be answered in the book. Write up three examples (demonstrating using the question mark) and, using the contents and index pages, see if the book is likely to answer them.

Reading, steady, write Give each pair of children a non-fiction title. Ask them to write a question on their whiteboards that might be answered in the text. Tell them to pass their whiteboards and book to another pair who should check in the book to see if the question is answered. Take in the results.

Use the acetate to add 'these texts answer questions' to the Big Book chart under the heading 'Non-fiction'.

INDEPENDENT READING

Give each group a selection of fiction and non-fiction books. Tell them to decide whether the text is fiction or non-fiction and write evidence to support their choice.

Introduce a non-fiction text at an appropriate level for the group. Ask them to predict whether it is fiction or non-fiction and to check off on a list whether it has specific features. Begin reading and discuss the purpose of the different features as the children come to them.

PLENARY

Display the targets for this unit. Read through, talking about the types of things the children will be doing to help them meet the targets.

Reinforce learning from this session. Go back to Big Book *Features* and complete the list of characteristics of each genre.

SESSION (2)

FOCUS

- **What are the contents, index and glossary for?**

RESOURCES

- Essential Non-fiction Anthology *Contents and index pages; Skateboarding* glossary pages 4–5
- Resource Sheet 1 *Headings and Definitions* (cut into strips)
- Selection of non-fiction books, containing glossaries

SHARED READING

Time out for thinking Ask the children to work with a partner and to remember as many features as they can about the structure of non-fiction texts.

Look together at the contents and index pages in the Anthology, and discuss how they are linked.

Ask the children to work in pairs to find non-fiction texts that have glossaries. (Alternatively, discuss the short skateboarding glossary on page 5 of the Anthology).

Bring the children back together to discuss their findings. How are the glossaries organised? Are they on a page all together or in a box related to a section of the text? How are the words explained in the glossary identified in the text? Explain that a glossary often has technical or unfamiliar vocabulary. Help the children to decipher any unfamiliar words by blending the phonemes.

Choose a topic, e.g. football or the Romans. Ask the children to suggest specific vocabulary that would need to be included in a glossary. Talk about the language of definitions (and remind them about the dictionary they looked at in Session 1).

Write Contents, Index and Glossary on the board, allocate random sentence strips from RS1 to individual children, and ask them to decide which heading to put them under.

SENTENCE WORK

Draw an outline of a hand and write a question word (*Who? What? When? Where? Why?*) for each finger. Explain that 'Why?' will give an answer using 'because'; 'When?' will give an answer about time; 'Where?' will give an answer about place; 'Who?' will give an answer about a person or animal.

Point at a question word and then at a child who has to quickly say a question starting with that question word.

Write the following sentence on the board: *Kim crept into the cave*. Explain that 'Who', 'What' and 'Where?' are answered by the sentence. Tell them to extend the sentence to answer the questions 'Why' (*because she was hiding from her brother*) and 'When' (*after she heard her brother call*). Write some of their suggestions on the board.

(Links with GfW Unit 3.)

INDEPENDENT READING

Write the following sentences on the board *The teacher smiled at the children. The monster burst into tears. The cat jumped on to the wall.* Ask the children to extend them by answering the questions *Why?*, *When?* and *Where?*. Encourage them to try out the sentences orally and then write them on a whiteboard, working with a partner if they need support.

⊙ **Extension** challenge the children to devise complex sentences which answer all the 'Wh-?' questions, e.g. *Last night*, (When) *at the circus* (Where) *the boy* (Who) *laughed at the silly clown* (What) *who fell over* (Why).

GUIDED READING — CORE

Introduce a non-fiction text at an appropriate level. Ask each child to devise one question that they expect this book to be able to answer. Review the questions at the end of the session.

PLENARY

Play '20 Questions' to reinforce the children's ability to compose questions. Think of something and tell the class if it is an animal, a person or something you can eat, etc. Challenge the children to guess it by asking a maximum of 20 questions. You can only answer 'yes' or 'no'.

SESSION 3

FOCUS

● **What are the language features of non-fiction texts?**

RESOURCES

● Non-fiction Skills Big Book Pages 2–3 *Features;* page 4 *First Day;* page 5 *Victorian Schools*
● Resource Sheet 2 *Fiction or Non-fiction?*

WORD WORK

Adding 'ing' Ask the children why we add 'ing' to words (*to form adjectives or verbs*). Demonstrate some actions (e.g. *walking, smiling, and sitting*) and ask the children to guess what you are doing. Write each word on the board at the top of a column. Ask them what they notice about the effect of adding 'ing' to a base word.

Invite individual children to come out and to mime an action for the rest of the class to guess. Write the base word on the board and ask pupils in pairs to write the word with its 'ing' ending on their whiteboards. Check that the children understand the rules about changing the spelling of the base word. *(Links with SpB page 23.)*

SHARED READING

Read the fiction text *First Day* on p.4 of the Big Book. Ask the children if the text is fiction or non-fiction. How can they tell? (*tells a story, characters, dialogue, past tense, pronouns*). Read the non-fiction text on the facing page and ask how they can identify it as non-fiction (*present tense, impersonal, layout, facts, impersonal pronouns*). Using the acetate sheet label the different features.

INDEPENDENT READING

Give out the sentence strips (RS2). Tell the children to work with a partner (mixed ability) to decide if the sentence comes from a fiction text or a non-fiction text. They should divide their whiteboards into two columns and write the number of each sentence strip in the correct one. They should pass around the strips until everyone has allocated all 12 sentences.

GUIDED READING — EXTENSION

Select a non-fiction text at an appropriate level. Introduce it and read parts of it. Ask the group to think about what it would be like if it was a work of fiction. Ask them to compose a first sentence of a fiction book on the same theme, demonstrating the difference in style.

PLENARY

Share the findings of the independent work. Play 'In the dock'. Invite pairs of children to defend why they positioned a sentence in a category. Draw conclusions about the language features of information texts (*present tense, impersonal, etc.*) Add this information to the chart on pp.2–3 in the Big Book.

SESSION 4

FOCUS

- **Can you recognise the book and language features of non-fiction texts?**

RESOURCES

- Non-fiction Skills Big Book pages 2–3 *Features*
- Essential Non-fiction Anthology pages 2–5 *About Skateboarding;* pages 6–7 *Pride Comes Before a Fall*

SHARED READING

Explain that you are going to read a fiction and non-fiction text on the same subject.

Listening focus What are the advantages and disadvantages of each type of text as a way of finding out about skateboarding?

Read the non-fiction text about skateboarding. Select specific vocabulary that may be problematic and demonstrate how to use grammar to work out unfamiliar words. Check characteristics against the *Features* in the Big Book. Use the Question Hand (introduced in Session 2) to record some of the information that they have found out from reading the text.

Read the fiction text about skateboarding. Ask the children in pairs to find examples of typical text and language features. Help them to make comparisons with the non-fiction text. Draw out the idea that each text has a different purpose and audience.

Ask the children which text they like better. Why?

INDEPENDENT READING

Tell the children to work with a partner and to think up 10 book titles – 5 fiction titles and 5 non-fiction (e.g. *'Bees', 'The Lazy Bee'*).

Extension provide children with a selection of fiction and non-fiction texts on the same subjects. Ask them to read the opening page and note down what they think are the intended audience and purpose of the book.

GUIDED READING · SUPPORT

Select a non-fiction text at an appropriate level for the group. Involve the children in noticing the features of non-fiction as they read. Ask them to devise a fiction book title for a book on a similar theme. What types of differences would they expect to find when they started to read?

PLENARY

Share independent work and invite children to challenge their peers to identify which title is fiction and which is non-fiction. Consolidate children's understanding of the features of fiction and non-fiction and relate this to the idea of purpose and audience.

SESSION 5

FOCUS

- **Can you write in the style of a fiction or non-fiction text?**

RESOURCES

- Non-fiction Skills Big Book pages 2–3 *Features*
- Resource Sheet 1 *Headings and Definitions*
- Resource Sheet 3 *Changing Notes into Sentences*
- Resource Sheet 4 *Contents and Index*
- Examples of sentences from Session 3 independent work
- Range of non-fiction texts
- Essential Non-fiction Anthology

SHARED WRITING

Teacher scribing Have one of the sentences from RS2 (used in Session 3) written on the board before the Session and add some brief notes, e.g. *Shark's teeth grow in rows. (Notes: 3000 teeth at a time; teeth drop out; deadly hunters…)*

Ask the children to identify whether the sentence comes from fiction or non-fiction. Explain that you are going to write a sentence to follow the one on the board. Look together at the notes and ask the children to suggest ways of turning the notes into sentences. Talk about sentence boundaries as you write and involve the children in deciding where full stops and capital letters are needed. (See RS3 for examples).

Read the finished sentences through together. What characteristics of non-fiction writing have you used?

Supported composition Ask the children to repeat this process with another sentence from RS3. Talk about the notes and how the words and phrases can be transformed into sentences. Children compose orally and then write their sentences down.

INDEPENDENT READING

Remind the children about the purpose of contents and index. They then answer the questions on RS4, using their Anthologies.

GUIDED READING · CORE

Working with a selection of non-fiction texts explore with the group how contents and index pages may vary in different publications. What essential features remain the same? Refer to the definitions created in Session 2 with RS1. Evaluate the effectiveness of the contents and index for each book.

PLENARY

Check the children's understanding of contents and index pages by reviewing the activities. Share answers to RS4 completed in independent work. Invite members of the core group to share their findings on the range and variety of contents and index pages.

SESSION ⑥

🔍 FOCUS

- **How can you identify the important facts in a text?**

RESOURCES

- Non-fiction Skills Big Book pages 6–7 *Over the Phone*
- Essential Non-fiction Anthology pages 8–9 *Welcome to Alton Towers*
- Resource Sheet 5 *At the Wildlife Park*

SENTENCE WORK

Introduce the idea that information can be presented in an attractive and interesting way in order to hold the reader's attention and get a message across. Look together at the pages about Alton Towers in the Anthology. Ask the children to identify the purpose and audience for the text *(to let visitors know about the attractions and help them plan their visits)*.

Ask the children how the information is made to look attractive *(use of colour, vivid, dramatic photos, amusing artwork, enticing headings)*. Explain the importance of all the text and graphic features *(e.g. bold, size of print, capitalisation, italics, headings, unusual font)*. Why these attractive styles have been chosen?

SHARED READING

Read the telephone conversation between the boy and his grandmother (Big Book pp.6–7). Discuss how much you learn about the theme park. Using the acetate sheet, mark the text which gives specific information about it. Imagine you wanted to go there. What extra information would you need? *(location, cost, opening times, etc.)* Jot these down as questions *(e.g. Where is the theme park? What time does it open?)*

INDEPENDENT WRITING

RS5 contains a child's oral account of a trip to a wildlife park. Tell the children to mark the text where there is specific information. Tell them to devise three questions about the park which are not answered in the text *(e.g. Can you feed the animals?)*

GUIDED WRITING ⎯ EXTENSION

Mark the information on RS5 and discuss how to organise this information into headings for a brochure *(e.g. Places to eat, Animals to see)*.

PLENARY

Talk about a trip you have been on. Include some facts and some anecdotes. Tell the children to jot down the main facts about your outing. Look at some examples. Did everybody note the same facts? How could you present this information for somebody who wanted to plan a similar trip?

SESSION ⑦

🔍 FOCUS

- **How can you use a spidergram to record essential facts?**

RESOURCES

- Essential Non-fiction Anthology pages 8–9 *Welcome to Alton Towers*
- Resource Sheet 6 *Graphic Designs*
- Brochures from tourist attractions

SHARED READING

Read and discuss the information about Alton Towers. Show the children a blank spidergram and explain its purpose.

💭 **Time out for thinking** Ask the children to work in pairs and to select five headings for the main sections of the spidergram (e.g. *rides, how to find it, places to eat, cost, opening times*).

Share the children's ideas, ensuring that they understand how a main section may have many subsections *(rides would include kids' rides, water rides, white-knuckle rides, etc.)* Enter the information on to a spidergram. Ask the children to advise you where each item of information should go. (Save the spidergram for subsequent sessions.)

SENTENCE WORK

Look again at the information about Alton Towers in the Anthology. Write the following headings on the board: *bold, all capitals, italics, underlined, enlarged, other interesting typefaces*. Ask the children to find examples.

Share their examples and discuss how the information was designed to be read. Distribute examples of brochures from tourist attractions. Discuss the presentation of information and ask the children to identify any examples of the features they have just been looking at. Draw out the idea that these print features are used for a specific purpose.

Links to GfW Unit 5.

INDEPENDENT WRITING

Give out RS6. Ask the children to present the information in a more exciting way using some of the features discussed in shared work *(bold, capitals graphic design, etc.)*

GUIDED WRITING ⎯ SUPPORT

Give pairs a brochure and ask them to cut out examples of different ways of presenting text *(bold, italics, capitals, typefaces, etc.)* Stick onto a large sheet and discuss the various options for presenting text attractively.

PLENARY

Using the Question Hand and the spidergram prepared earlier see how many of the questions about the theme park can be answered *(What is it? A theme park with rides for all ages)*.

SESSION 8

FOCUS

- **How can you transform data from prose to diagram?**

RESOURCES

- Essential Non-fiction Anthology pages 10–11 *Alton Towers: All you need to know!*
- Resource Sheet 7 *Adding -ing*

SHARED READING AND WRITING

Read Anthology pages 10–11. Study the chart about the distances to Alton Towers. Look at the map. Ask the children which motorways you would need to travel on if you lived in Sheffield and wanted to get to Alton Towers. Explain that you are going to convert information presented in prose into different diagrams. Demonstrate how to present the opening times information in a chart.

Time out for discussion Tell the children to read the section on costs, and then work with a partner to decide how to present this information in a chart. Discuss their suggestions.

WORD WORK

Time out for thinking Ask the children to talk to a partner and to recall three facts about adding 'ing' to verbs.

Write *asking* on the board and invite the children to say how it adds '-ing'. Does it (1) just add 'ing', (2) drop 'e' before adding '-ing', or (3) double the consonant after its short vowel before adding '-ing'? Write the following verbs on the board and ask the children to write down the base words: *hopping, hoping, smiling, walking, running, pulling, meeting, taking, coming, shopping*. Work as a class to sort the verbs into the three categories they represent. *(Links to SpB, page 4.)*

INDEPENDENT WRITING

Give each group of 6 a copy of RS7 cut up into cards. Tell them to work in teams of 2. Place the word cards face down on the table. Taking turns, each team looks at a card and writes down the word with its '-ing' ending. When all the cards have been turned over, the teams check each other's answers on the answer sheet and add up their scores *(two points for right answers, none for wrong ones)* to see who has won.

GUIDED WRITING — CORE

Review the children's presentation of information about costs from the whole class session. Devise questions together about costs and determine whether the information has been included on the chart. Edit.

PLENARY

Review the independent work. Take in the scores from the groups. Were any words particularly tricky? Discuss with the class which category each word belongs to.

SESSION 9

FOCUS

- **How can you use graphic design to enhance the text in your own leaflets?**

RESOURCES

- Non-fiction Skills Big Book pages 8–9 *World of Adventures*
- Copies of a thesaurus

WORD WORK

Ask the children to recall the features of a dictionary and to make comparisons with a thesaurus. Give groups a thesaurus to look at. Reinforce the idea of alphabetical order and play a game involving finding a word quickly. Demonstrate the purpose of the thesaurus by demonstrating how to find alternatives for the word 'good'.

SHARED WRITING

Talk for writing Tell the class they are going to write part of a leaflet about a theme park. Look at the illustration in the Big Book. The children should think of a name for their park and names for the rides that will attract visitors. Explain that they will be writing a brief description for each ride. Remind them about using headings, side headings, capitals, underlining and graphic design to make their leaflet enticing.

Brainstorm with the class some vocabulary to describe the rides *(plunges, twists, splashing, adventure, futuristic, phantom, magical, exciting)*.

Teacher scribing Choose one of the rides and discuss with the class a suitable name and description (e.g. *A scary ride called 'Phantom Nightmare' in wobbly writing to make it look spooky. This is ride is only for the brave!*) Explain that you are writing facts about the rides, but making them sound exciting to persuade people to come to the theme park.

EXTENDED INDEPENDENT WRITING

Tell the children to choose a name for their theme park, to name the rides and to write about each one. Suggest they turn their pages sideways and fold them, to look like the inside page of a leaflet. Remind them of the structure: sub-heading with name of ride followed by sentences giving details. Encourage them to use a dictionary and thesaurus as they write.

GUIDED WRITING — SUPPORT

Ask each child to select one ride to write about. Give time for oral composition before writing and encourage children to help one another revise and improve their ideas. Put the information together to produce a single leaflet for the group.

PLENARY

Invite the children to read out the name and description of one of their rides. Ask others how tempted they would be to go on that ride. Encourage the children to explain how they presented their words.

SESSION ⑩

🔍 FOCUS

● **How can you present information more clearly?**

● **What have you learnt in this unit of work?**

RESOURCES

● Resource Sheet 8 *My Reading Preferences*
● Class thesaurus

WORD WORK

Select some of the sentences that the children have used to describe the rides. Discuss with the class whether other words might have made the ride sound more exciting. Demonstrate how a thesaurus can provide alternative linked words (e.g. *a child may have written 'You'll get wet on this ride.' The thesaurus might suggest 'soaked' or 'drenched'*).

💭 **Time out for thinking** Ask pairs of children to find exciting alternatives for words used in their leaflets e.g. 'great'. (Explain that not all entries are suitable, e.g. *great* can mean *severe* if we talk about a great pain.)

Discuss with the class how to display their leaflets most effectively.

SHARED READING

Introduce RS8 and read it through with the children. Ask them to think about the last few books they have read (at home as well as at school). Ask them which section they choose their books from when they go to the library and if they have favourites at home.

INDEPENDENT WORK

Give each child a copy of RS8 'My Reading Preferences'. Ask the children to work with a partner and to discuss their answers before completing the questionnaire.

GUIDED WRITING — SUPPORT

Ask the group to think about their favourite books and whether they prefer fiction or non-fiction. Draw up a tally chart and record preferences under fiction or non-fiction. Record girls' and boys' preferences separately.

EXTENDED PLENARY: REVIEW AND EVALUATION

Complete the tally chart for the whole class. Divide the class into 'fiction supporters' and 'non-fiction supporters'. Ask 2 confident children to present their preference for fiction or non-fiction and to try to persuade the others to read their favourite book.

Display the targets for this unit and read through with the children. Have we reached our targets? What do we know about identifying fact and fiction? What have we learned about different ways to display text? Help the children to think about the evidence in their own work and reflect on their own progress.

INTERACTIVE CD

On the Literacy World Interactive CD for Stage 1 Non-fiction, you will find the following resources for this unit:

● Copies of all the Non-fiction Skills Big Book pages for this unit for interactive work (*Features Checklist* pages 2–3, *First Day* page 4, *Victorian Schools* page 5, *Over the Phone* pages 6–7 and *World of Adventures* pages 8–9)

● An audio recording of *Over the Phone*

● A short video clip of an advert for Thorpe Park

● Interactive word and sentence work for Sessions 3, 7, 8 and 10

● All the Resource Sheets for independent work for you to customise

● Comprehensive Teaching and Planning Guides for the unit are also available on the CD.

Headings and Definitions

✂

Contents
Index
Glossary
Appears at the front of the book
Lists the main topics in the book
Gives a page reference for the topic
Appears at the end of the book
Lists all topics in alphabetical order
Gives all page references for all the topics
Appears at the end of the book
Words in **bold** in the text are listed here in alphabetical order
Explains the meaning of words written in bold type

STAGE 1 | TERM 1 | For use with Unit 1 Session 2: Shared reading

Fiction or Non-fiction?

1. Strawberries are soft, red fruit which grow on small plants close to the ground.

2. 'I'll just eat one more strawberry,' thought Connor, 'she'll never know.'

3. The shark swam closer. Jack could see its cold grey eyes as it circled the boat.

4. Sharks' teeth grow in rows. When a tooth drops out the next tooth behind moves forward to replace it.

5. Some spiders spin webs to catch their prey.

6. The sticky cobweb brushed against Lucy's face and she gave a little squeal.

7. Then Daniel saw the wasp land on the old man's bald head. 'What do I do now?' he thought desperately.

8. Wasps are insects with yellow and black stripes. The wasp protects itself with a sting.

9. The spaceship sped onward at light speed. 'I hope we reach Jupiter in time,' thought Captain Blake.

10. The planet Jupiter is 778 million kilometres from the sun.

11. The world's highest waterfall is the Angel Falls in South America.

12. 'We must stop the boat,' yelled Adam, ' I can hear a waterfall ahead.'

Changing Notes into Sentences

Example of sentences from non-fiction:

Original sentence:

Shark's teeth grow in rows. When a tooth drops out the next tooth behind moves forward to replace it.

Notes to use when writing further facts:
- *3000 teeth at a time*
- *teeth drop out*
- *deadly hunters*

Example of an additional sentence which uses further facts and maintains the impersonal style:

At any one time the shark may have up to 3000 teeth in its mouth.

Further examples:

Original sentence:

Some spiders spin webs to catch their prey.

Notes:
- *web made of sticky strands*
- *insects get stuck*

Additional sentence:

The web has sticky strands and insects cannot fly away once they have landed on the web.

Original sentence:

Strawberries are soft, red fruit which grow on small plants close to the ground.

Notes:
- *farmers put straw under plants*
- *fruit rots when it gets wet*

Additional sentence:

Farmers put straw underneath the plants so that the strawberries are not touching the wet ground. That would make them go rotten.

Example of a sentence from fiction:

Original sentence:

The shark swam closer. Jack could see its cold grey eyes as it circled the boat.

Notes:
- *builds up sense of tension*
- *eyes seem to be sending a message*

Additional sentence which includes features of fiction (use of personal pronouns, describing feelings, making shark appear to have human thoughts):

The eyes seemed to be saying, 'There's no escape. I can get you whenever I want.'

Contents and Index

Use the contents and index pages of the Non-fiction Anthology to answer the following questions.

1   Where would you look in a book to find the index?

    _____

2   Write out three main headings found in the contents.

    _____

3   How did you know these were main headings?

    _____

4   Why is the index given in alphabetical order?

    _____

5   On what page would you learn about Roman Gladiators?

    _____

6   Would you look in contents or index for information about African elephants?

    _____

7   Where will you learn 'Key Facts about Hippos'?

    _____

8   Where would you look in the book to find information about 'Hobbies'?

    _____

9   Where would you look in the book to find information about a specific hobby, e.g. skateboarding?

    _____

10 Why aren't the contents of a book in alphabetical order?

    _____

At the Wildlife Park

Underline the facts

Last summer we went to Longslade wildlife park. First we drove through the monkey park. I thought it was dead good but Mum got stressed when a monkey climbed up on the bonnet and ripped off the windscreen wiper!

Then we went into the lion park. A big notice told us not to stop and not to wind down the window. We could see some lions asleep under the trees. We wanted to get a closer look but Mum said it was too dangerous to stop, so we drove on. After that we parked the car and ate our picnic in the picnic area. Mum said there would be long queues in the café but we could get an ice cream from the ice cream van.

Then we went to the seal show. It was dead funny. The seals could do all sorts of tricks.

We went on a bit and saw a man feeding the penguins. He let some children throw fish for them but I didn't want to because the fish smelled horrible.

There was a big queue at the end because it closed at 6.00 and everyone was leaving at the same time.

Think of 3 more things that would be useful to know about the wildlife park that you do not know.

1. _____

2. _____

3. _____

Graphic Designs

Choose two pieces of information about Longslade and make them look as attractive as you can.

Longslade Wildlife Park for a great day out.

Play ball with the sea lions.

100 different flavours of ice cream.

Fun for all the family for only £25.

Adding -ing

To be photocopied onto card and cut out – one set (with answers) for each group.

Answers

smiling	taking	asking	writing	looking	jumping
saying	hopping	making	riding	drinking	clapping
shutting	driving	walking	helping	coming	going
doing	wasing	meeting	eating	thinking	seeing

✂

hop	make	clap	walk	meet	see
write	say	wash	help	do	think
ask	jump	drink	drive	go	eat
smile	look	ride	shut	come	take

My Reading Preferences

Which do you like best – fiction or non-fiction?

1. I like reading _____ best because _____

    Or

    I like reading both fiction and non-fiction because

    _____

2. Things I like about fiction

    _____

    _____

3. Things I don't like about fiction

    _____

    _____

4. Things I like about non-fiction

    _____

    _____

5. Things I don't like about non-fiction

    _____

    _____

6. My favourite books

    _____

    _____

STAGE 1 | TERM 1 | For use with Unit 1 Session 10: Independent work

© Harcourt Education Ltd. 2004. Copying permitted for purchasing school only. The material is not copyright free.

1 1 2 Non-chronological Reports

KEY INFORMATION

TEACHING OBJECTIVES

TEXT LEVEL

T1 T19 to locate information, using contents, index, headings, sub-headings, page nos and bibliographies.

T1 T20 to compare the way information is presented, e.g. comparing a variety of information texts including IT based sources

T1 T21 to read information passages, and identify main points or gist of text, e.g. by noting or underlining key words or phrases, listing the 4 or 5 main points covered.

T1 T23 to write simple non-chronological reports from known information, using notes made to organise and present ideas; write for a known audience

SENTENCE LEVEL

T1 S9 to notice and investigate a range of other devices for presenting text

T1 S13 to use commas to separate items in a list
Grammar for Writing Unit 7

WORD LEVEL

T1 W5 to identify misspelt words in own writing; keep spelling logs; learn to spell them

T1 W13 to collect new words from reading

T1 W14 to infer the meaning of unknown words from context

UNIT SUMMARY

RESOURCES

- **Essential Non-fiction Anthology** *About Elephants; Key Facts About Hippos; Mighty Mammals; Snake spidergram; Crocodiles*

- **Non-fiction Skills Big Book** *What are Report Texts?; About Elephants; Writing frame; Spidergram for Snakes; Crocodiles*

- **Resource Sheets** 1–9

- **Literacy World Interactive** Unit 2

In this two- or three-week unit the children read examples of non-chronological reports and learn about the structure and language features of this text type. They research topics, make notes and present the information in their own non-chronological reports.

The optional third week offers further reinforcement of the key objectives.

5–14 GUIDELINES

Reading level B and B/C
- Reading for information
- Awareness of genre
- Knowledge about language

CHILDREN'S TARGETS

READING

I know how information is organised in a non-chronological report.

I can find out information from different types of text. (*Week 3*)

WRITING

I can make notes and use them to write a non-chronological report.

I can present the information in the form of a non-chronological report. (*Week 3*)

SENTENCE

I can use charts to present information.

WORD

I can work out the meaning of a word.

SPEAKING AND LISTENING

I can present information clearly.

WIDER CURRICULUM LINKS

The skills developed in reading and writing reports apply to other subjects, especially History and Geography.

Literacy World GUIDED READING LINKS

- *Incredible Insects* (Core and Satellites)

OUTLINE PLAN

SESSION	WHOLE CLASS WORK		INDEPENDENT WORK	GUIDED GROUPS	WHOLE CLASS WORK plenary
1 Monday	**Shared reading** Brainstorm elephants then read BB text on elephants looking for features of non-chronological reports		**Independent reading** Use the question hand to devise 5 questions about elephants that can be answered from the BB text	**Guided reading** (support) Look at features of a non-chronological report **RS1**	What do we want to achieve in this unit? We'll use what we learn to make a class reference book
2 Tuesday	**Shared reading** Discuss layout and purpose of headings, etc, in the Elephant report in the Anthology. **T19**	**Word work** Use context to decode unfamiliar words Collect vocabulary relevant to topic – mammals, carnivores, etc **W13 W14**	**Independent writing** Comparison chart – Decide if statements are true or false **RS2**	**Guided writing** (extension) Using information from library books, devise a chart to log differences between animals	Can you remember some key facts about elephants?
3 Wednesday	**Sentence work** Group sentences to form paragraphs using **RS3** (*GfW9*)	**Shared writing** Plan report on hippo based on facts in Anthology using BB writing frame. Model writing first paragraph **T23**	**Independent reading** Pick out key details from Anthology text on hippos using question hand	**Guided reading** (support) Collect fresh information about hippos from external sources	Can you insert fresh information into your report?
4 Thursday	**Shared writing** Demonstrate writing paragraph on habitat of hippo **RS4**	**Extended independent writing** Children write one further paragraph about hippos		**Guided writing** (support) Rehearse sentences aloud before writing about hippo's food	Class questions 'panel of experts' on hippo facts
5 Friday	**Word work** Collect vocabulary for the topic, arrange in alphabetical order, link to glossary **S9**	**Shared reading and writing** Use **RS5** to plan turning information into a report **T21**	**Independent writing** Children work to improve shared example of poor report **RS5**	**Guided writing** (support) Discuss how to improve the writing on **RS5**	**Editing** Take in suggestions from independent work and edit text
6 Monday	**Word work** Play 'Stand up–Sit down' when nouns are heard	**Shared reading** Read examples from Anthology and look at different ways of writing reports **T20**	**Independent reading** Children examine a range of different texts to see which are non-chronological reports **T20**	**Guided Reading** (core) Look at less common examples of reports	Share findings from Guided group. What differences did we find in the range of report texts?
7 Tuesday	**Sentence work** Revise nouns – play 'Granny went to Market'. Insert commas in a list **S13** (*GfW7*)	**Shared reading** Read Big Book spidergram on snakes. Demonstrate how the notes form the basis of a report **T23**	**Independent writing** Using another source add more information about snakes	**Guided reading** (extension) Use IT to find more information about snakes	Add notes to class spidergram from independent work
8 Wednesday	**Shared writing and sentence work** Demonstrate turning notes on spidergram into non-chronological report		**Independent writing** Create a labelled diagram to add to their report **S9**	**Guided writing** (support) Extract information from spidergram	Can you compare different styles of presentation and say which is easiest to access?
9 Thursday	**Sentence work** Common nouns and proper nouns using commas in a list **S7**	**Shared reading** Demonstrate making further notes from different sources **T21**	**Independent writing** Write report text for remaining paragraphs about snakes **T23**	**Guided writing** (core) Create a glossary	Guided group share glossary on snakes
10 Friday	**Shared writing** Review main features of report text Draw writing frame **T23**	**Extended independent writing** Children write fair copy of their report about snakes modelled on BB writing frame **T23**		**Guided writing** (support) Provide writing frames with headings to help with organisation	Have we achieved our targets for this unit?

Abbreviation key	**GfW**	Grammar for Writing
	SpB	Spelling Bank
	RS	Resource Sheet

SESSION	WHOLE CLASS WORK		INDEPENDENT WORK	GUIDED GROUPS	WHOLE CLASS WORK plenary
11 Monday (optional)	**Shared reading** Brainstorm (KWL) crocodiles. Read text in BB and discuss different ways of presenting information **T20**		**Independent reading** Children label a picture of a crocodile, using information from Anthology **RS6**	**Guided reading** (core) Research information in library books or ICT. Make notes **T21**	A rare chance to be a crocodile! Can you answer questions about your life style?
12 Tuesday (optional)	**Shared reading and note-taking** Read anthology text and ask children to make notes **T21**	**Word work** Look at 10 common misspellings and discuss ways to counteract them **W5**	**Independent reading** Spelling generalisations using **RS7**	**Guided reading** (extension) Find more information using Internet or CD-ROM	Discuss rules governing spellings
13 Wednesday (optional)	**Shared writing and sentence work** Working on report writing frame in BB, demo first paragraph of Crocodile report using **RS8, RS9**		**Extended independent writing** Children write own reports on crocodiles **T23**	**Guided writing** (support) Rehearse sentences aloud before writing	Discuss language features of reports
14 Thursday (optional)	**Shared writing** Discuss different ways of presenting reports. Demo presenting charts, maps, etc **T20**		**Extended independent writing** Complete reports using writing frames and planning notes – add illustration **T23**	**Guided reading** (core) find illustrations and diagram	Check punctuation and spelling and edit completed reports
15 Friday (optional)	**Review and evaluation** Review what they have learnt about writing reports. Provide book to hold their reports		**Independent writing** Assign tasks around the edges of the class book – creating contents list and index, designing the cover	**Guided writing** (core) Support where necessary	How has making this book met our targets?

Abbreviation key
GfW Grammar for Writing
SpB Spelling Bank
RS Resource Sheet

TEACHING NOTES

SESSION (1)

FOCUS

- **What are the features of a non-chronological report?**

RESOURCES

- Non-fiction Skills Big Book pages 2–3 *Features*; pages 10–11 *What are Report Texts?*; pages 12–13 *About Elephants*
- Resource Sheet 1 *Features of Report Texts*
- Non-chronological reports on other animals

SHARED READING

? Limbering up What are the features of non-fiction texts. Draw together their ideas. (See lists on Big Book pp. 2–3).

Introduce this new unit of work and make links with previous work on non-fiction. Remind the children there are different types of non-fiction text. In this unit they will read and write non-chronological reports about different kinds of animals, and turn their reports into a class book.

Have a brainstorm about elephants, and note key words and phrases. Read the Big Book report. Compare the facts in the report with those on the brainstorm.

Display the Big Book list of features of non-chronological reports and look for examples in the shared text. Mark them on the acetate sheet. Make links between the features and the way that information is presented (e.g. *the purpose of a labelled diagram; the reason for using bold type for headings*).

INDEPENDENT READING

Remind children of the Question Hand (introduced in Unit 1). Ask them to draw a hand and think of 5 questions that this text answers about elephants.

GUIDED READING — SUPPORT

Look together at the features of non-chronological reports listed on RS1. Cut it up into strips and give each child 2 strips. Read a suitable non-chronological report text (alternatively, you could reread the elephant text in the Big Book). Help children to link their strips to specific examples in the text.

PLENARY

Introduce the targets for the unit. Explain that the children will be reading examples of reports and then researching and writing their own. Introduce the idea of a class reference book about animals that everyone will be able to read and use. Ask the guided group to demonstrate how they linked the feature strips to text examples. Ask the rest of the class to decide whether they agree.

SESSION ②

FOCUS

- **Can you identify and use further features of a non-chronological report?**

RESOURCES

- Essential Non-fiction Anthology pages 12–13 *About Elephants*
- Resource Sheet 2 *Comparing Elephants*
- Non-chronological reports on other animals

SHARED READING

Read Anthology pp 12–13.

◁) **Listening focus** What additional information can we learn about elephants from this text?

Draw attention to the further features of this text not seen in the Big Book version. Talk about the purpose of headings, side headings, illustrations, diagrams, maps, and discuss reading strategies (e.g. starting with the heading, then scanning the whole page and returning to the main text before looking in detail at the illustrations).

Ask the children what they have found out about different types of elephant. Draw two columns on the board headed *African Elephant* and *Asian Elephant*. Ask the children to think about the different features of the elephant's appearance that you can compare, and enter them as headings for each row (e.g. *ears, trunks, foreheads, tusks*). Ask the children to supply information for each column. Explain a chart is the best way to compare information. *(Links with GfW, Unit 9)*

WORD WORK

Identify specific vocabulary in the shared text. Explain that non-fiction texts often include specialised technical vocabulary relating to a particular subject. Discuss strategies for reading and understanding the words in context and make a note of key words (e.g. *herbivores, Africa, mammals, habitat, trunk, matriarch*). Discuss the spelling as you write.

INDEPENDENT WRITING

Read through each statement on pages 12–13 in the Anthology and decide whether it is true or false for each type of elephant. Record findings on RS2.

GUIDED WRITING — EXTENSION

Using a non-chronological report on other animals (such as pets or wild animals) ask the children to help you devise a chart to show key differences. Discuss what information to include on the chart, and whether presenting information in a chart makes it easier to read.

PLENARY

Have a quiz on elephant facts, based on the children's independent work. Read out some of the statements and ask children to identify whether they are about African or Asian elephants.

SESSION ③

FOCUS

- **How do you organise information in a non-chronological report?**

RESOURCES

- Non-fiction Skills Big Book pages 14–15 *Writing Frame for Animal Report*
- Essential Non-fiction Anthology pages 12–13 *About Elephants;* pages 14–15 *Key Facts About Hippos*
- Resource Sheet 3 *Hippo Factsheet*
- Resource Sheet 4 *Hippo Report*

SENTENCE WORK

Write the word *hippo* on the board. Brainstorm with the class some information they know about hippos and note any key words and phrases. Encourage them to compose questions if they are not sure about the facts (e.g. *Do they eat other animals or just plants?*)

Read the statements about hippos (RS3, cut into strips) and give them out to pairs of children. Explain the information can be arranged into a non-chronological report with a paragraph for each category of information. Write the following headings on the board, one above the other but with space between: *Habitat, Appearance, Food.* Ask each pair to come out in turn and place their sentence under the correct heading. *(Links with GfW Unit 9.)*

SHARED WRITING

Planning for writing Look at Anthology pp.14–15 and explain that this gives detailed facts about hippos, but that it is not sorted in any way. Explain that you are going to use these facts to write a non-chronological report about hippos. Demonstrate how to read part of the text, identify a key fact and note it under a heading (habitat, appearance or food).

Introduce the writing frame (Big Book pp.14–15) and point out that the headings are similar to those used for *About Elephants* (Anthology pp.12–13). Reread the first paragraph about the elephant and remind children that this is an opening definition that introduces the subject. Point out that the information under each sub-heading corresponds to a paragraph.

Demonstration writing Model composing an opening definition for the first paragraph. It should include specific or technical vocabulary, an impersonal style with generalised participants and use the present tense. (See RS4 'Hippo Report' for exemplar shared writing text). Keep this work to use in Session 4.

INDEPENDENT READING

Remind the children that non-fiction texts answer questions. Recap some useful question words (e.g. *What? Where? When? Why? How?*) Tell them to draw a Question Hand and label the fingers. Ask the children to read through all the information on Anthology pp.14–15 about hippos, and write one question about it for each question word.

Collect information from a website or library books about hippos. Support the children in identifying specific information. Can they find five more facts about hippos?

PLENARY

Invite individual children to choose one of their questions for the other children to answer. Can the support group add further information with the new facts they discovered? Which category could the new notes be added to?

SESSION 4

FOCUS

- **Can you write in the style of a non-chronological report?**

RESOURCES

- Essential Non-fiction Anthology pages 14–15 *Key Facts About Hippos*
- Non-fiction skills Big Book pages 12–13 *About Elephants*
- Resource Sheet 4 *Hippo Report*

SHARED WRITING

Look back through the information collected in the previous session, categorised under different headings. Refer to the hippo information in the Anthology.

Demonstration writing Read through the opening definition written in the previous session. Write the next paragraph about hippos using all the available information. Refer again to the Big Book (pp.12–13). Demonstrate writing the next paragraph on the hippo's habitat (see RS4). Discuss how you can take a single word or phrase from the notes and turn it into a sentence.

Supported composition Discuss what will be included in the paragraph on appearance. Ask them to select facts for their first sentence, and rehearse orally before writing.

EXTENDED INDEPENDENT WRITING

Tell the children they are going to complete the paragraph about appearance and go on to write a paragraph on food. They should use the sentences on the board and information from the Anthology to help them. Remind them to sustain the formal language of reports.

🔁 **Extension** Children who complete these paragraphs can go on to write a final paragraph (e.g. *about why the species is under threat, or other interesting hippo facts*).

GUIDED WRITING — SUPPORT

Ask the children to identify further information to include under Appearance. They should orally rehearse what they want to say before writing, and continually reread to check for sense. Discuss the paragraph on food together. Scribe an opening sentence and support the children as they continue to write independently.

PLENARY

Play 'Ask the Expert'. Choose four children to be a panel of expert naturalists. Tell them that they can use the information in the bullet point text in the Anthology and the shared writing. Invite others in the class to ask them questions (e.g. *Why are hippos' ears on the tops of their heads? Are hippos carnivores?*).

SESSION 5

FOCUS

- **Can you improve a piece of writing using the features of a non-chronological report?**

RESOURCES

- Non-fiction Skills Big Book pages 10–11 *What are Report Texts?*; pages 14–15 *Writing Frame for Animal Report*
- Resource Sheet 5 *Report on Tigers*
- Dictionaries
- Reference books about tigers

WORD WORK

Ask the children to help you to select key vocabulary for a glossary for the 'Hippo' text. Write the suggested words onto word cards and display on the board (e.g. *herbivores, mammals, grazing*). Ask the children to rearrange the words into alphabetical order. Discuss definitions, involving children in using the dictionary to check the meaning of unfamiliar words.

SHARED READING AND WRITING

Shared reading Read RS5 to the children. Ask for their comments drawing out the way the paragraph has not been presented in the style and language of a non-chronological report.

Planning Look back at the checklist of features of non-chronological reports and ask the children to help you amend the example. *(Add headings and sub-headings: definition, habitat, appearance, food; group similar information together; avoid personal comments; provide more facts; use technical vocabulary, etc.)* Go through the list of facts and discuss ways of categorising the information under different headings. Look at the text and distinguish between facts and opinions/descriptions/ unnecessary details.

Teacher scribing Look back at the writing frame (Big Book pp.14–15) and talk about using the same structure to present this information. Ask the children to suggest a heading and ideas to include in the opening definition. Write this, incorporating the children's ideas. Emphasise the use of formal language (e.g. *Instead of 'attractive to look at' write 'Tigers are mammals. They are members of the big cat family'*).

INDEPENDENT WRITING

Ask the children to work on RS5 with a partner to continue to rewrite the information in the style of a report, using the same headings as the writing frame in the Big Book.

⊃ **Extension** Children could go on to use reference books to research information about tigers in fresh categories to extend their reports.

GUIDED WRITING — SUPPORT

Work with the group to read the text and to discuss how it could be improved. Refer to the checklist of features in the Big Book (page 11).

PLENARY

Take in the children's suggestions for improvements and complete the new version of the text on tigers. Refer back to the checklist – does this new version have all the features? Is there anything else that needs to be added or changed?

SESSION 6

FOCUS

- **Can you recognise common features in different types of report?**

RESOURCES

- Non-fiction Skills Big Book pages 10–11 *What are Report Texts?*
- Essential Non-fiction Anthology pages 16–17 *Mighty Mammals*
- Resource Sheet 1 *Features of Report Texts*
- A range of non-chronological texts

WORD WORK

Check that the children know what a noun is by playing 'Stand up/Sit down'. Read a passage of text to the class. When they hear a noun they should stand up. Ask them to identify which word prompted them to stand. List the nouns on the board.

SHARED READING

? Limbering up How many features of non-chronological reports can you remember? Take feedback and refer to the list of features in the Big Book to remind children of previous learning.

Explain that not all non-chronological reports will follow the layout of the 'elephants' text. Read the examples from the Anthology (pp.16–17) and talk about similarities and differences. Emphasise the audience and purpose of each one and use the checklist of features. Give children copies of RS1 to check for specific features. Talk about the fact that the texts do not all have every feature.

INDEPENDENT READING

Divide children into small mixed ability groups. Provide a wide range of different non-chronological texts (*leaflets, library books, internet texts, guidebooks, magazine articles*) for groups to determine how many features of non-chronological reports each text demonstrates. They should select one text at a time and check it against the criteria (on RS1).

GUIDED READING — CORE

Support the group to explore some of the less common examples of non-chronological reports (e.g. *guidebooks or texts on the Internet*).

PLENARY

Share the findings about the different report texts. Make comparisons between the different texts and ask children which had the most features on the list and which had the least. Discuss these questions: *How few features does a text need and yet still be a non-chronological report? Are some features essential? Are some optional? Can they think of other examples of non-chronological reports?*

SESSION 7

FOCUS

- **Can you collect information for a non-chronological report about a particular type of animal?**

RESOURCES

- Non-fiction Skills Big Book pages 10–11 *What are Report Texts?*; pages 16–17 *Snakes*
- Selection of non-fiction books about snakes
- Access to ICT facilities

SENTENCE WORK

Play a few rounds of 'Granny went to market…' (*…and bought, apples, bananas, Corn Flakes, dates, eggs, fish, grapes*). Write each item on the board as it is added. Talk about the items being nouns (naming words). Explain how we can often recognise a noun because it comes after words like 'a' 'the' or 'some'. Demonstrate how to separate the items in the list by using commas.

(Links with Grammar for Writing, Unit 7)

SHARED READING

? Limbering up Think of three questions about snakes to answer. Take feedback and note some of the most interesting or original questions.

Introduce the idea of writing a report on snakes for a class book on animals. Explain that you will need some source material with facts about snakes. Turn to pp16–17 in the Big Book. Can they remember what this type of chart is called? *(spidergram)*. Begin to read through, drawing attention to the way the information is presented and contrasting this with a report (e.g. *bullet points and notes rather than complete sentences arranged in paragraphs*).

Involve the children in identifying specific facts, making use of the features of the spidergram.

Talk about using this information in a report – challenge the children to compose complete sentences orally using some of the facts from the spidergram.

INDEPENDENT READING

Children read another source of information about snakes and continue to make notes, categorising the information in the same way as on the spidergram.

GUIDED READING — EXTENSION

Use an ICT source to research further information about snakes, e.g. a CD-ROM encyclopedia. Point out features that help you with this type of text *(video clips, links to other subjects, sound, etc.)*

PLENARY

Take feedback from the independent task and add further notes to the spidergram. Keep it for Session 8.

SESSION 8

FOCUS

- **How do you turn notes into a non-chronological report?**

RESOURCES

- Non-fiction Skills Big Book pages 14–15 *Writing Frame for Animal Report;* pages 16–17 *Snakes*

SHARED WRITING AND SENTENCE WORK

Refer back to the information on the spidergram. Tell the children that you are going to turn the notes into a non-chronological report for the class book on animals.

Demonstration writing Using the non-chronological writing frame in Big Book pp.14–15, demonstrate writing the information for two sub-headings *(opening definition* and *habitat)* paying particular attention to the language features of reports. Draw attention to the way that each sentence in the paragraph relates to the heading. Refer to the notes and involve the children in composing sentences that use specific words from the spidergram.

Ready, steady, write Invite the children to work in pairs to transform the data on the spidergram into a 3rd paragraph about what snakes eat. Ask two children to have their work ready to discuss in the plenary.

INDEPENDENT WRITING

Remind the children that information can also be presented in a labelled diagram. Draw a simple diagram of a snake on the board for the children to copy. Ask them to label the skin, ears, eyes, fangs and poison using the information on the spidergram. Keep these diagrams for use in Session 10.

GUIDED WRITING — SUPPORT

Work with the group to help them extract the information from the spidergram to complete the labels for their snakes.

PLENARY

Share the work completed by the two children. Examine how language is used differently in report texts, spidergrams and labelled illustrations. Which information is the easiest to read? Which is the most interesting?

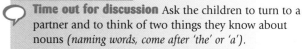

SESSION 9

FOCUS

- **Can you use the features of a report in your own writing?**

RESOURCES

- Non-fiction Skills Big Book pages 16–17 *Snakes*
- Essential Non-fiction Anthology pages 18–19 *Snakes*

SENTENCE WORK

Time out for discussion Ask the children to turn to a partner and to think of two things they know about nouns *(naming words, come after 'the' or 'a')*.

Take in their ideas and draw attention to the difference between common nouns and proper nouns. Brainstorm a list of animals found in a zoo. Write the names on the board and discuss placing the commas to separate the nouns in a list. Tell them to omit the comma after 'and' at the end of a list.

SHARED READING

Review the information that has already been included in the report on snakes: opening definition, habitat, food and appearance (labelled diagram) and start to collect additional information for the remaining paragraphs.

Read through Anthology, pages 18–19. Ask the children to pick out the information on 'breeding', 'killing prey' and 'interesting facts' . Demonstrate how to make notes and add to the spidergram (e.g. by attaching post-it notes to the Big Book page).

INDEPENDENT WRITING

Ask the children to write the remaining paragraphs about snakes as report text. Remind them that they are writing to inform and interest their peers. They should refer to the checklist of criteria to ensure they sustain the appropriate level of formality in the language.

GUIDED WRITING CORE

Help the group to select appropriate words from the spidergram and the completed report text to create a glossary. Remind the children about the form (alphabetical order) and purpose of a glossary. Monitor and support as they use dictionaries to find definitions.

PLENARY

Invite the core group to share their work on a glossary about snakes. Have they defined all the technical language? Are there any other words that should be added?

SESSION 10

FOCUS

- **Can you present information on snakes in the form of a non-chronological report?**

RESOURCES

- Non-fiction Skills Big Book pages 12–13 *About Elephants*; pages 16–17 *Snakes*
- Labelled snake diagrams (completed in Session 8)

SHARED WRITING

Briefly review the text and language features of reports. From their work on snakes so far ask the children to identify specific examples of the features. Discuss what they should include in a report on snakes. Draw out a writing frame with heading and each sub-heading listed *(opening definition, habitat, appearance (labelled diagram), food, killing prey, breeding, interesting facts)*. Refer to the Big Book pages on elephants to remind the children what a finished report looks like, pointing out that you have added some additional features *(diagram, more categories of information)*.

💬 **Time out for discussion** Ask the children to work with a partner and to think of a title for their report.

EXTENDED INDEPENDENT WRITING

Ask the children to make a final version of their report about snakes following the writing frame and using the information from the last three sessions. Encourage them to think about illustrations, diagrams, charts, etc. They can present their reports in their best handwriting, or use ICT if practicable.

GUIDED WRITING SUPPORT

Provide a writing frame with headings for each part of the report. Support the children in identifying the relevant information from the spidergram and talk about how to include their labelled diagram. Prompt them to compose sentences orally before writing.

PLENARY

Display the targets for the unit and read through each one. Ask the children to reflect on the work that they have done and the sort of evidence it provides. Look back at all the features they used in their completed reports.

SESSION 11 OPTIONAL

FOCUS

- **How can you find out about crocodiles and make notes on a spidergram?**

RESOURCES

- Non-fiction Skills Big Book pages 10–11 *What are Report Texts?*; pages 18–19 *Crocodiles*
- Essential Non-fiction Anthology pages 20–21 *Crocodiles*
- Resource Sheet 6 *Crocodile!*
- Access to ICT facilities
- Library books

SHARED READING

Planning Brainstorm prior knowledge about crocodiles, and jot down the information in note form. Structure it under the following headings: *Definition, Food, Habitat, Appearance, Breeding, Amazing fact*. Ask the children if there is any more they would like to know about crocodiles.

Read the information in the Big Book. Compare it with the class brainstorm. Identify further facts and add to the list.

Talk about the different ways information can be presented for different purposes. Review some forms used earlier in the unit (e.g. *labelled diagram, map, chart for making comparisons*) and talk about the advantages of each one.

INDEPENDENT READING

Ask the children to complete RS6 with information from the Anthology.

GUIDED READING CORE

Give the group a selection of non-fiction books about crocodiles and also access to information from ICT sources. Make notes about new information gleaned.

PLENARY

Hot seat the crocodile! Choose a child to be the crocodile. Invite other children to ask it questions (e.g. *What do you eat? Do you give birth to live young?*)

SESSION (12) OPTIONAL

FOCUS

- **What strategies can you use to remember how to spell tricky words and new vocabulary?**

RESOURCES

- Essential Non-Fiction Anthology pages 20–21 *Crocodiles*
- Resource Sheet 7 *Spelling Generalisations*

SHARED READING AND NOTE-TAKING

Read the text in the Anthology again. Ask individuals to pick out one or two important or interesting points about crocodiles. Challenge the other children to write the information in note form. Compare notes and discuss how these fit into the categories used for notes in Session 11.

WORD WORK

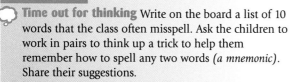 **Time out for thinking** Write on the board a list of 10 words that the class often misspell. Ask the children to work in pairs to think up a trick to help them remember how to spell any two words (*a mnemonic*). Share their suggestions.

Extend the range of learning strategies (e.g. *talk about using the word meaning, or the word root to link with other words that might help spelling*). Talk about breaking words into syllables to help identify where vowels might be needed. Also suggest mispronouncing words in order to hear hidden phonemes.

Revisit vocabulary relevant to the topic of wild animals and discuss ways to categorize them according to sub-headings (*food, habitat, etc.*) or according to alphabetical order, number of phonemes or word with prefixes.

INDEPENDENT READING

Distribute RS7 and tell the children to study the text on crocodiles in the Anthology, find examples of each of the spelling generalisations and fill in the Resource Sheet.

GUIDED READING — EXTENSION

Set the group the challenge of carrying out further research using a website or CD-ROM encyclopedia. Talk about the different reading strategies needed for specific sources. Monitor their ability to identify relevant information and make notes.

PLENARY

Collect in the examples children found of the spelling generalisations. Discuss the rules which govern the spellings.

SESSION (13) OPTIONAL

FOCUS

- **How can you turn your notes into a report text?**

RESOURCES

- Non-fiction Skills Big Book; pages 14–15 *Writing Frame for Animal Report;* pages 18–19 *Crocodiles*
- Essential Non-fiction Anthology pages 20–21 *Crocodiles*
- Resource Sheet 8 and 9 *Crocodile Report*

SHARED WRITING AND SENTENCE WORK

Explain that you are going to write an entry for the class book about animals. This will bring together information collected from all the different sources you have used. Using the writing frame in Big Book pp.14–15, show the children how the sub-headings relate to the different categories used for the notes on crocodiles.

Demonstration writing Write the introductory paragraph defining what a crocodile is. Remind the children that sentences in a paragraph must be on the same theme and take their ideas for sentence boundaries and punctuation. (See RS8 and RS9.)

EXTENDED INDEPENDENT WRITING

Ask the children to begin writing their own reports on crocodiles using the writing frame in the Big Book. They should refer to the class planning notes completed in previous sessions, the information in the Anthology and also to their own labelled illustration. Invite two children to write their reports for discussion in the plenary. Those who do not finish can carry on in the next session.

GUIDED WRITING — SUPPORT

Help the children to organise their ideas into the formal language of reports through oral rehearsal before writing. Children need to consider whether it 'sounds like an information book'. Prompt them to make changes based on the examples they have read.

PLENARY

Share the reports written by the two children for discussion. Cross-reference with the text and language features in the Big Book and talk about ways to make the writing 'sound more like a report'. Have they included all the relevant facts? Involve the children in suggesting changes or additions.

SESSION 14 OPTIONAL

FOCUS

- **How can you present your report in a way that engages the reader?**

RESOURCES

- Demonstration writing completed in Session 13

SHARED WRITING

Remind the children about the various ways of presenting information they have learned in this unit. Look back at the plan for the Crocodiles report. Could the information be presented in a different way to make it easier to understand? (e.g. *a labelled photograph to display alongside the text about appearance; a map showing where crocodiles can be found; a chart comparing alligators and crocodiles.*) Select one idea and use it to demonstrate.

EXTENDED INDEPENDENT WRITING

The children complete their reports using the writing frame and planning notes. They read through what they have written, checking for accuracy and sense. If they have time they can add an illustration or diagram to their text.

GUIDED READING CORE

Challenge these children to find illustrations or diagrams that they could use in their reports. Support them as they search for information on relevant websites, e.g. *National Geographic*. Talk about the type of ICT and reading skills needed to locate and sift information.

PLENARY

Ask the children to work in pairs checking punctuation and spelling in one another's completed reports. Support them in identifying errors and noting corrections. Take feedback about common mistakes.

SESSION 15 OPTIONAL

FOCUS

- **What have you learnt about non-chronological reports?**

RESOURCES

- Non-fiction Skills Big Book pages 10–11 *What are Report Texts?*
- Children's completed reports

REVIEW AND EVALUATION

Preparation Before the Session, prepare a class book (e.g. from large sheets of sugar paper), number the pages and put in the completed reports on different animals. Tell the children they are going to put all the information about wild animals into a book.

Review all the stages leading up to the writing of a report – *the brainstorm (What do we know? What do we want to know?); spidergram (sorting out the key headings and paragraphs for a report); research and note-taking; labelling diagrams (getting the facts right); checking against the criteria for report writing; writing each paragraph in turn ensuring that the relevant facts hold together; keeping the language formal.*

Display the list of features of non-chronological reports and ask children to read through their own report on crocodiles. Ask them to reflect on the features they have included and the style they have used. Do they feel more confident about writing in this style now? Were they able to include information from a range of different sources?

INDEPENDENT WRITING

Ask the children to refine their reports so that they are ready for inclusion in the class book. Remind them to think about the organisational devices the book will need (*contents, index, glossary, etc.*) and assign children to put these together.

PLENARY

Assemble the book, adding the contents, index, illustrations, glossary. Look through it together and reflect on what has been achieved.

Literacy World
INTERACTIVE CD

On the Literacy World Interactive CD for Stage 1 Non-fiction, you will find the following resources for this unit:

- Copies of all the Non-fiction Skills Big Book pages for this unit for interactive work (*Features Checklist* pages 2–3, *What are Report Texts?* pages 10–11, *About Elephants* page 12–13, *Writing Frame for Animal Report* pages 14–15)
- Short video clips about elephants, hippos, tigers and crocodiles
- Interactive word and sentence work for Sessions 3, 5, 6 and 12
- All the Resource Sheets for independent work for you to customise
- Comprehensive Teaching and Planning Guides for the unit are also available on the CD.

Text characteristics

Heading
Sub-heading
Opening definition
Technical vocabulary
Information about habitat
Information about appearance
Information about food
Unusual fact
Non-chronological

Language characteristics

Present tense verbs
Does not give give the name of a particular animal But refers to the whole species
Action verbs
Precise language
Formal style

Name _____ Date _____

Comparing Elephants

1. **Read the information about elephants on pages 12-13 of the Anthology.**
2. **Compare the appearance of African and Asian elephants.**
3. **Read each statement and decide whether to tick or cross.**
4. **Add more statements to compare their habitat.**

	African elephants	Asian elephants
Large fan-shaped ears	✓	✗
One lip on trunk		
Smaller triangular-shaped ears		
Two lips on trunk		
Generally larger		
Generally smaller		
Males have tusks, but not females		
Rounded forehead		
Two bulges on forehead		

Hippo Factsheet

Hippo facts for the children to group under Appearance, Diet and Habitat.

Hippos are large mammals.

Male hippos weigh up to 3200kg.

Hippos can be as long as 4 metres.

Their ears, eyes and nostrils are on the tops of their heads.

They have short legs.

They have enormous jaws and huge teeth.

Hippos are herbivores.

They eat grass and other plants.

They graze on riverbanks.

They leave the water to feed at night.

Their name means 'river horse'.

They spend all day in the cool of the water.

Hippo Report

Hippos

Hippopotamuses (usually called hippos) are <u>large animals</u>. Male hippos weigh up to 3200 kg and grow up to 4 metres long. The word 'hippopotamus' means 'river horse' and hippos spend most of the day in rivers.

> Find a more accurate word – '<u>mammals</u>'.

> Add further information (in a 3rd sentence) that relates to the general definition.

Habitat

<u>Hippos</u> live in rivers and lakes in East and West Africa. <u>They</u> are becoming rarer because people hunt them.

> Demonstrate how to write about generalised participants rather than specific animals.

Appearance

<u>Hippos</u>' ears, nostrils and eyes are on the top of <u>their</u> heads so they are above the surface of the water while the rest of the body and the head stay below. This means <u>the hippo</u> can keep as much of its body as possible in the cool water during the heat of the day.

Food

Hippos are <u>herbivores</u>. They eat grass and other plants. In the cool of the evening they leave the river and graze on the river bank.

Literacy World

Report on Tigers

Key information to be used to improve the poor report below.

Tiger facts

- Large mammals
- Members of the cat family
- Found in India, China, Indonesia and Siberia
- Live in forests or jungle
- Fur – golden-orange with black markings
- Siberian tiger has pale coat – known as 'white' tiger
- Powerful legs – can leap up to 10m
- Sharp teeth, strong jaws
- Carnivores
- Eat deer, buffalo
- Hunt alone at night

Tigers

Tigers are very attractive to look at. They have orange and black fur but some of them have fur which is more white. They have big teeth and live in hot countries. They like to eat deer or sometimes buffalo. They can climb up quite high and run quite fast. I saw a good programme on the TV about tigers last week. I wouldn't like to meet a tiger because it might eat me.

Crocodile!

Label this illustration of a crocodile.

Tough, leathery skin

Spelling Generalisations

**Read the text on Crocodiles and find
examples of each of these spelling generalisations.**

**Adding 'ed' or 'ing' to words with a
long vowel and ending with a consonant**

_____   _____

_____   _____

**Adding 'ed' to a word with a short vowel and ending with
a consonant**

_____   _____

Adding 'ed' or 'ing' to words ending in 'e'

_____   _____

Adding the suffixes 'ly' or 'ful'

_____   _____

Changing 'y' into 'ies'

_____   _____

Crocodile Report

Crocodiles

Introduction paragraph identifies what a crocodile is

Crocodiles are reptiles. That means they are cold-blooded animals. In order to have the energy to hunt and eat crocodiles must absorb the warmth of the sun to raise the temperature of their blood. Crocodiles bask in the sun on the riverbank. To help control their temperature they open their mouths and appear to be yawning. At night they return to the river with only their nostrils and eyes above the surface.

Habitat

Crocodiles are found in rivers and lakes in warm parts of the world.

Appearance

Crocodiles range in size from 1.5 metres to 6.0 metres. A large crocodile can weigh over a tonne.
Crocodiles have thick leathery skin, short legs with webbed feet and a long snout. The snout of a crocodile is narrower than that of the alligator, which has a broad, rounded snout. Crocodiles have powerful jaws and rows of sharp pointed teeth. The 4th tooth on lower row sticks outside the jaw when the mouth is closed. This makes the crocodile look as though it is smiling. Crocodiles have an oar-like tail that they use to propel themselves through the water.

Correct use of full stops to create sentence breaks

Crocodile Report (cont'd)

Food

Crocodiles usually eat fish, turtles and crabs but a large Nile crocodile can attack and eat deer, hyenas, baboons and even hippos. Occasionally mature male crocodiles will attack humans.

Use of commas to break up a list

All sentences in paragraph are on the same theme

Breeding

The female lays 25 – 80 eggs. She digs a hole in the riverbank and sits on the eggs for their 3-month incubation period. The male hovers around to scare off predators. When the hatchlings are born they are approximately 30cm in length. The female carries them down to the water in her mouth.

Use information from the Big Book to shape language into report style

Amazing fact

When the eggs are ready to hatch the parents roll the eggs on their tongues to help the hatchlings break free from their shells.

Use to provide a model – the children will find their own amazing facts

1 2 3 Instructions

KEY INFORMATION

TEACHING OBJECTIVES

TEXT LEVEL

T2 T12 to identify the specific purposes of instructional texts

T2 T13 to discuss the merits and limitations of particular instructional texts, including IT and other media texts and to compare these with others, where appropriate, to give an overall evaluation

T2 T14 to understand how written instructions are organised

T2 T15 to read and follow simple instructions

T2 T16 to write instructions … and use writing frames as appropriate for support

SENTENCE LEVEL

T2 S9 to experiment with deleting words in sentences to see which are essential to retain meaning and which are not *GfW Unit 13*

T2 S10 to understand the differences between verbs in the first, second and third person,…collecting and classifying examples…relating to different types of text… *GfW Unit 14*

T2 S11 to understand the need for grammatical agreement in speech and writing

WORD LEVEL

T2 W4 to discriminate syllables in reading and spelling

T2 W6 to use independent spelling strategies

T2 W7 to practise new spellings regularly by Look, Say, Cover, Write, Check

UNIT SUMMARY

RESOURCES

- **Essential Non-fiction Anthology** *How to Make a Twizzer; How to Make a Balancing Bird; How to Play Tiddly-winks*
- **Non-fiction Skills Big Book** *The Magic Wood; How to Get to the Museum; Funny Face Biscuits; Beautiful Bathing*
- **Resource Sheets** 1–6
- **Literacy World Interactive** Unit 3

In this two-week unit the children read a range of different types of instructional texts, compare the presentation and identify common features. They have experience of following different types of instructions and writing their own.

5–14 GUIDELINES

Reading level B
- Reading for information
- Awareness of genre
- Reflecting on the writer's craft

CHILDREN'S TARGETS

READING

I can read and follow a set of instructions.

WRITING

I know how to write instructions.

SENTENCE

I know to use the second person when writing instructions.

WORD

I know different ways to learn spellings.

SPEAKING AND LISTENING

I can follow oral instructions.

WIDER CURRICULUM LINKS

Links to:
- Design and Technology
- Art and Design

Literacy World GUIDED READING LINKS

- *Making the Past into Presents* (Core and Satellites)

47

OUTLINE PLAN

SESSION	WHOLE CLASS WORK		INDEPENDENT WORK	GUIDED GROUPS	WHOLE CLASS WORK plenary
1 Monday	**Oral work** Brainstorm instructions e.g. school rules, recipes, route finders. Give children directions for moving around the room. Discuss features of the instructions **T12**		**Independent writing** Using whiteboards, in pairs work out a route for a friend to move around the classroom.	**Guided writing** (support) Orally prepare instructions	What do we want to in this unit? Practise following directions from independent work. Start class checklist
2 Tuesday	**Word work** Break polysyllabic words on the BB map of the Magic Wood into syllables **W4**	**Shared reading** Explain features of BB map of Magic Wood (compass, etc). Direct them to follow a route through the wood **T15**	**Independent work** Children sit back to back and give directions to partner **RS1**	**Guided writing** (extension) Write instructions for getting to school	Guided group read directions for rest of class to follow
3 Wednesday	**Sentence work** Look at ways to clarify directions by deleting unnecessary words **S9** (GfW 13)	**Shared reading** Discuss with class ways of making BB long-winded instructions clearer. Rewrite **T14**	**Independent writing** Write directions from the classroom to a specific area in the school **T16**	**Guided reading** (core) Look at texts that play with the format of instructions using rhyming words and lists	We can make instructions clear by listing them in order
4 Thursday	**Sentence work** Continue work on reducing sentences for instructions (GfW13)	**Shared reading** Read instructions in Anthology pp21-25. Add features to class check list **T14**	**Independent reading** Make either twizzer or Balancing Bird and evaluate instructions **T15 T16**	**Guided reading** (core) Look at further examples of instructions	Children demonstrate their models and discuss problems with instructions
5 Friday	**Spelling strategies** Discuss different strategies for learning spellings **W6**	**Shared writing** Demonstrate how to write instructions for making a model	**Independent writing** Children write instructions for others to follow; then check how well they worked **T15**	**Guided reading** (extension) Look at manufacturers' instructions	Class discuss ideas for making instructions clearer
6 Monday	**Shared reading** Review features of instructions. Discuss how to read a recipe **T14**	**Independent reading** Ask each group to follow instructions and make a biscuit face **T16**		**Guided writing** (core) Write the method for making icing	Discuss similarities and differences between recipes and directions
7 Tuesday	**Shared reading and writing** Divide the class into 2 teams and follow the illustrations for playing Tiddlywinks in the Anthology. Demonstrate writing instructions for the first two illustrations **T16**		**Independent writing** Finish writing instructions for playing Tiddlywinks using **RS3 T16**	**Guided writing** (support) Help with writing instructions	Share ideas for illustrations to clarify instructions
8 Wednesday	**Sentence work** Look at verbs used in instructions.	**Oral work** Discuss how to write a recipe for a Perfect Bath. Display the ingredients as a list **S10** (GfW Unit 14)	**Independent writing** Work with partner to devise ingredients for a Perfect Bath	**Guided writing** (core) Ask children to explain why they selected certain ingredients	Groups share ideas and create a list
9 Thursday	**Shared writing and sentence work** Demonstrate how to write the method part of your recipe using **RS5 T16**		**Independent writing** Children complete their Perfect Bath recipes by adding the 'method' **RS6**	**Guided Reading** (extension) Explore different ways the recipe format can be used	Individual children in the 'hot seat' describe their ideas for a Perfect Bath
10 Friday	**Word work** Discuss any problem spellings and ways that help to remember them **W6**	**Extended independent writing** Children make fair copies of their recipes taking care over spelling and presentation. They illustrate and label the features **RS6 T16**		**Guided Writing** (support) Check and discuss first drafts and final presentation	Have we met our targets for the unit? What have we achieved? How shall we display our work?

Abbreviation key
GfW Grammar for Writing
SpB Spelling Bank
RS Resource Sheet

TEACHING NOTES

SESSION ①

FOCUS
- **What are the features of instructions and rules?**

ORAL WORK
Explain to the class that in this unit they are going to learn how to read and write instructions and rules.

💬 **Time out for discussion** Ask the children to turn to a partner and to think of rules they have to obey (e.g. *at school, at home, on the road*). Share the children's examples.

Ask the children if they can notice any differences between the oral rule and the written rule by saying some out loud, and then writing them down (e.g. *'Please would you tidy the books on your desks' becomes 'Keep your desk tidy'*).

Explain that rules are very direct and usually start with a verb.

Ask the children to work in pairs to identify the verbs in all the sentences. Invite volunteers to come out and underline the verbs.

Explain that instructions are a set of rules that tell people how to make or do something. Discuss the children's experience of following instructions. Get them moving by playing some rounds of 'Simon Says'.

Ask selected children to follow instructions for moving around the room. Draw attention to the time sequence words (*e.g.* **First** *come out to the front.* **Next** *take two steps forward.* **Then** *turn to your right.* **Now** *take one step forward. Turn to your left.* **Finally** *take one step back*).

Review on the format and features of rules and instructions. Can the children describe the difference between rules and instructions? (*Rules direct you to do or not do something; instructions direct you how to do something*).

INDEPENDENT WRITING
Working in pairs, ask the children to write a set of instructions for another pair to move around the classroom and collect a specific object.

GUIDED WRITING — SUPPORT
Work out instructions with the group to collect a specific object. Scribe the instructions and ask them to identify the time sequence words and the verbs. Write these onto separate cards and ask the children to practise the spellings using Look, Say, Cover, Write, Check.

PLENARY
Invite pairs of children to read out their sets of instructions for individual children to follow. Do they get to the specific object? Are the instructions clear? Start a class checklist of the features of instructions and rules.

SESSION ②

FOCUS
- **Can you give directions for someone else to follow?**

RESOURCES
- Non-fiction Skills Big Book pages 20–21 *The Magic Wood*
- Resource Sheet 1 *The Magic Wood*

WORD WORK
Study *The Magic Wood* in the Big Book. Choose a place name (e.g. *'Whispering glade'*). Show the children how to divide the words into separate syllables *(Whis/per/ing)*. Write it on the board with oblique lines between each syllable. Explain how this helps with reading and spelling. Select other place names and ask the children to count the syllables and to record the number. They can then try spelling each syllable and checking their accuracy.

SHARED READING
Study the details of the map and explain the purpose of the compass. Ask the children which parts of the wood look the most interesting. Give directions for a route through the wood, and ask a child to mark the route on the acetate sheet. Then ask another child to devise directions for you to follow. (e.g. *I want to get to the giant's cave and I'm entering the wood from the north. Which direction must I go in?*) Draw out the importance of giving short, clear, accurate directions.

INDEPENDENT WORK
Give each child a copy of RS1. Tell the children to work in pairs and to sit back to back. While one child describes their journey through the wood, marking it on RS1, the other child marks the route on their own copy. Remind them to use the compass points and to use imperative verbs to start each instruction.

GUIDED WRITING — EXTENSION
Tell the group to work in pairs and to choose a route through the wood. They should write their instructions as accurately as they can, using time sequence words and imperative verbs, and finish their instructions by asking 'Where am I now?'

PLENARY
Invite the pairs from the guided group to dictate their instructions for the other children to mark on their Resource Sheets. Does everyone end up in the right place?

Refer to the class checklist of features of instructions. Do any features need refining or elaborating?

49

SESSION ③

FOCUS
- **Can you write directions concisely?**

RESOURCES
- Non-fiction Skills Big Book pages 22–23 *How to Get to the Museum*
- *Don't forget the bacon* by Pat Hutchins (Puffin)

SENTENCE WORK

Practise deleting unnecessary words in the following sentence to make the instructions clearer: *Melt the chocolate – you could buy milk chocolate or white chocolate but white chocolate looks a bit pale with the Rice Krispies – in a pan – if you use a non-stick pan it will be easier but you must use a wooden spoon not a metal spoon because that will scratch the pan.* Discuss with the children where long sentences are appropriate and where short sentences are best. Discuss this in relation to writing instructions. *(Links to GfW Unit 13.)*

SHARED READING AND WRITING

Read *How to Get to the Museum* in the Big Book (pp.22–23) as the children follow.

◁) **Listening focus** How easy would it be to follow these directions?

Discuss with the children how successful the directions are. Ask them to help you to underline the important words. Do they need to add any information to make them clearer, e.g. distances, direction, left or right?

Demonstration writing Rewrite the directions using bullet points, time sequence words and imperative verbs. Read through the new directions and compare them to the class checklist. Do they fulfil all the criteria? Is there anything that needs adding to the checklist?

INDEPENDENT WRITING

Ask children to write a set of directions for a route from one part of the school to another (e.g. *from the classroom to the hall*). Remind them about *time sequence words, imperative verbs* and *bullets points or numbered points*. Encourage them to refer to the class checklist.

GUIDED READING — CORE

Either share with the group 'Don't forget the bacon' by Pat Hutchins (Puffin) or use jumbled items in a shopping list *(e.g. Six brown eggs could become six brown pegs; a cake for tea could become a rake for me; a pound of pears could become a pound of bears, etc.)*. Play around with the rhymes but end each verse with 'Don't forget the bacon'. The point of the story is that the boy repeats each item getting more confused, until he correctly recalls all the things but forgets the bacon.

PLENARY

Talk about the importance of keeping items in a list or directions clear.

SESSION ④

FOCUS
- **What do good instructions need?**

RESOURCES
- Essential Non-fiction Anthology pages 22–23 *How to Make a Twizzer*; pages 24–25 *How to Make a Balancing Bird*
- Resource Sheet 2 *Template for a Twizzer*
- Resource Sheet 3 *Template for a Balancing Bird*
- Materials and equipment listed in the Anthology instructions.

SENTENCE WORK

Return to the activity reducing sentences to essentials from the previous session. Peg the words of another sentence on a washing line and challenge the children to assess the effect of removing one word at a time (e.g. *Slowly and carefully, the clever child with red hair cut out the circle shapes that were drawn on the card*).

Does the sentence still make sense or has the meaning changed? Is it still a sentence? Look carefully at the words that have been removed and begin to hypothesise which classes of words can be removed without destroying the sense *(nouns and verbs are usually essential)*.

(Links with GfW Unit 13.)

SHARED READING

Read the two sets of instructions in the Anthology pp.21–25 *How to Make a Twizzer* and *How to Make a Balancing Bird*. Discuss with the class the similarities and differences between the two sets of instructions. Add to the checklist any features not already on the list *(e.g. headings, side headings, numbered points, bullet points, use of illustrations)*.

INDEPENDENT READING

Ask the children to choose whether they would like to make the Twizzer or the Balancing Bird. They should follow the instructions and note any parts of the instructions that were not clear.

GUIDED READING — CORE

Explore on the Internet further examples of sets of instructions (e.g. CBBC website instructions from one of the art programmes). Cross-refer the instructions with the class checklist and note any new features.

PLENARY

Invite children to demonstrate their completed models. Discuss any problems in following the instructions. Could anything have been made clearer? Ask the focus group to share the further examples they discovered on the web.

SESSION (5)

FOCUS

- **How can you devise clear instructions for building a model?**

RESOURCES

- 6 Lego bricks per pair
- Examples of instructions from construction kits

WORD WORK

Choose some words that the class find difficult to spell and write them on the board. Ask each child to select one they find hard and copy it on to a whiteboard, underlining the part they stumble over.

Time out for discussion Ask the children to think of strategies for learning spellings. Collect in the different suggestions and discuss where each one might be helpful (*e.g. syllabification (for longer words) separating phonemes, analogies, words within words, mnemonics*).

Demonstrate how to select a particular strategy to help with one of the difficult words and then ask each child to identify the strategy they could use to help learn their chosen word.

SHARED WRITING

Make a model using 6 Lego bricks of different colours and sizes. Do not show it to the class. Give a child an identical set of bricks and, using the formal language of instruction, tell them how to make a model just like yours. When they have finished, reveal your model. Are they the same? Were the instructions sufficiently clear? Could they be improved?

INDEPENDENT WRITING

Give each pair of children Lego pieces of various sizes. Ask them to construct a spacecraft using not more than 6 blocks. They should then write a set of instructions to make the model, referring to the class checklist. When the spacecraft is made, they should dismantle it and pass on the bricks and instructions to another pair, who read the instructions and build the model. They then pass the craft back to the original designers to see if it matches their specification. Did they manage to follow the instructions?

GUIDED READING — EXTENSION

Ask the children to read and compare some real examples of manufacturers' instructions for models. Ask them to make notes of the features. Help them spot the use of diagrams and the very small amount of written text.

PLENARY

Collect in suggestions for making the Lego instructions clearer (*e.g. more illustrations, more specific language*). Look at the instructions found by the guided group – what is the main difference from those written in the shared session (*use of diagrams*). If possible, display some instructions from construction kits. What do they notice? Why is it easier to use illustrations and diagrams? (*difficulty in describing different pieces, need to overcome language barriers*).

SESSION (6)

FOCUS

- **Can you read and follow a recipe?**

RESOURCES

- Non-fiction Skills Big Book pages 24–25 *Funny Face Biscuits*
- Ingredients and utensils as listed on the recipe

Preparation Before the lesson make the water icing (approximately 2 tbs water to 500g icing sugar). Mix well. Divide into 4 equal parts. Use a drop of different food colouring in each part (red, yellow and blue). Mix well. Drop a nozzle into each icing bag and spoon in the icing. (Or spoon the icing into a small plastic bag, place it inside another one, and make a small diagonal cut across one corner). Twist the bag to force the icing out of the hole.

SHARED READING

Time out for discussion Ask the children to talk with a partner about food they have made in the kitchen at home or at school and cookery programmes they have seen on the TV. Take feedback and talk about how they knew what to use and what they had to do. Introduce the word *recipe* and ask them to come up with a definition.

Show the class the *Funny Face Biscuit* recipe in the Big Book. Talk about the text organisation and the language features. Demonstrate to the children how to read a recipe and talk through how to follow the instructions (*e.g. importance of collecting all the ingredients and utensils before you start, reading through all the instructions before carrying out the first one*). Ask questions to check children's comprehension (*e.g. How much white icing will you need? What do you do with the blue icing?*).

INDEPENDENT READING

Give each group of children a set of the ingredients and materials. Tell them to follow the instructions and to make a biscuit face. As they are clearing up ask them to think about how useful the recipe was. Did it need clarifying? Was there enough information?

GUIDED WRITING — CORE

Talk to the children about the method for making the icing. Ask them to help you compose another recipe for this. Repeat the process, one step at a time, with the children making notes at each stage. Once the process is complete, compare the children's notes and talk about what would be included in the finished recipe.

PLENARY

Compare the biscuit faces. Who managed to follow the instructions accurately? Discuss the similarities and differences between recipes and directions and add any new information to the class checklist.

SESSION 7

FOCUS

- Can you follow instructions that are presented as a series of pictures?

RESOURCES

- Essential Non-fiction Anthology pages 26–27 *How to Play Tiddlywinks*
- Resource Sheet 4 *How to Play Tiddlywinks*
- Approx. 50 small and 8 large tiddlywinks
- 6 saucers or shallow bowls

SHARED READING AND WRITING

Look at pp.26–7 in the Anthology. This has a series of pictures depicting the instructions for playing tiddlywinks. Ask if anyone has ever played tiddlywinks. Do they know the rules?

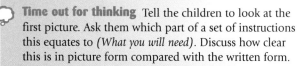

Time out for thinking Tell the children to look at the first picture. Ask them which part of a set of instructions this equates to *(What you will need)*. Discuss how clear this is in picture form compared with the written form.

Look at the remaining pictures. Do the children have a clear idea about how to play the game? Divide the class into groups of 4: two opposing pairs. Make available all the necessary resources but allow children to select what they need based on the instruction diagrams *(8 tiddlywinks of two colours per group; saucer)* Tell the children to follow the instructions and play the game. Move around the groups and check whether children are following the diagrams accurately *(do they have the right number of tiddlywinks; are they all playing behind a 'line'; are they taking turns?)*

Demonstration writing Draw the children back together and discuss what they found difficult to follow in the diagrams. Did they sort out the sequence of actions for playing the game? What difference would it make if there were written instructions to follow. Demonstrate how to turn the content of the first two pictures into written form: 'What you will need' and 'The game' (see RS4). Write these on the board discussing the layout and language features explored in the previous week.

INDEPENDENT WRITING

Tell the children to work with a partner and use RS3 to complete the instructions for playing tiddlywinks.

GUIDED WRITING — SUPPORT

Support this group as they write their instructions. Monitor their ability to use the format and language features of instructional writing, prompting as necessary.

PLENARY

Share ideas for instructions for illustrations 3–8. Check against class checklist. Draw out the idea that a combination of written instructions and pictures may be easiest to follow when you are learning the rules of a game.

SESSION 8

FOCUS

- Can you plan the ingredients for your own recipes?

RESOURCES

- Non-fiction Skills Big Book pages 26–27 *Beautiful Bathing*
- Essential Non-fiction Anthology pages 22–23 *How to Make a Twizzer*

SENTENCE WORK

Use one of the sets of instructions from previous sessions for a 'Collect and Classify' activity (e.g. *How to Make a Twizzer'* Anthology pp.22–23). Ask the children to find examples of verbs. Draw out the idea that they are written in the second person with the pronoun 'you' omitted. Talk about why instructions are written in this way.

(Links with GfW Unit 14.)

ORAL WORK

Show the class the Big Book picture of the luxurious bath (pp.26–27).

Time out for discussion Talk to a partner about which features of the bath look most appealing.

Explain to the class that you are going to use the format of a recipe to write about how to create your perfect bath. Go around the picture reading the labels to all the items. Brainstorm with the children which features they think you would most like. Explain that you will list their suggestions in note form which can be expanded later *(e.g. Ingredients: wash-away worries soap; body beautiful bubbles; youth-retaining shampoo. Utensils: wrinkle-reducing flannel, flattering mirror).*

INDEPENDENT WRITING

Tell the children to work with a partner and to select and list the ingredients and utensils for their own perfect bath.

GUIDED WRITING — CORE

Challenge the group to come up with some unexpected reasons for choosing certain ingredients *(e.g. choose the plastic ducks because they are really two-way radio).* Encourage them to add their own imaginative ideas.

PLENARY

Invite the guided group to share their ideas. List some of the suggestions other children have come up with under 'Ingredients'. Talk about spelling features of some of the more unfamiliar words. Make this list available for reference when children are completing their own recipes.

SESSION ⑨

FOCUS

- **Can you use the structure and language features of a recipe in your own writing?**

RESOURCES

- Non-fiction Skills Big Book pages 26–27 *Beautiful Bathing*
- Resource Sheet 5 *A Perfect Bath*
- Resource Sheet 6 *A Recipe for a Perfect Bath*

SHARED WRITING AND SENTENCE WORK

Talk for writing Refer back to the list of ingredients and utensils made in the previous session. Explain that you are going to write a 'method' that uses all these things. Ask children to discuss ideas and suggest instructions. Can they make it 'sound like a recipe' by using verbs in the second person at the beginning of each sentence? Summarise each step in brief notes to provide a basic plan.

Demonstration writing Begin writing the first step, rehearsing the sentence orally and then removing the pronoun to make it sound more like instructions. Incorporate specific items from the list of ingredients (see RS5). Involve the children in checking that you are using the language features and structure of a recipe.

Supported composition Ask the children to look back at their own lists of ingredients and to discuss the method for their own perfect bath. Support them in making brief notes so that they will be able to continue writing independently.

INDEPENDENT WORK

Ask the children to complete their recipes using their lists of ingredients and the notes they have made. Remind them to use the structure and language features of a recipe and to keep rereading their work to check for sense.

 Support Provide copies of the writing frame (RS6) for children who need help in organising this work.

GUIDED READING — EXTENSION

Look for further examples of authors using the instruction/recipe format in unexpected ways (e.g. *Recipe for a Disastrous Family Picnic* by Ian Souter Stage 1 Essential Fiction Anthology p.63; *Little Bo Peep's Library Book* by Cressida Cowell (Hodder)). Compare them with conventional recipes. Talk about the effect of using the format in a different way.

PLENARY

Invite children to sit in the 'hot seat' and talk about their perfect bath. They could give a running commentary about taking a bath *(e.g. I'm diving into the blissfully warm perfumed water. I am watching the tropical fish through the glass-bottomed bath as they swim around in the tank below)*.

SESSION ⑩

FOCUS

- **Can you check and revise your work and present it in a finished form?**

RESOURCES

- Resource Sheet 6 *A Recipe for a Perfect Bath*

WORD WORK

Write on the board any problem words that occurred in their first drafts *(e.g. water, bath, running)*. Talk about ways of learning how to spell these words *(e.g. Look, Say, Cover, Write, Check)*. Tell the children to work with a partner and to study the spellings on the board, then take turns to test each other, using their whiteboards.

EXTENDED INDEPENDENT WRITING

Give each child a copy of RS6. Tell them to make a fair copy of their recipe taking particular care over spelling and presentation. When they have finished writing they should draw the relevant features in their bath.

GUIDED WRITING — SUPPORT

Support the children in reading through their first drafts and checking them for meaning, punctuation and spelling. Monitor their ability to identify errors and support them in making corrections. Talk about how they will present their finished work using RS6. Provide an ICT option, if available.

PLENARY

Discuss with the children how to present their finished pieces of work. How would they like them to be displayed?

Review the main teaching points of the unit and talk through the unit targets.

Literacy World
INTERACTIVE CD

On the Literacy World Interactive CD for Stage 1 Non-fiction, you will find the following resources for this unit:

- Copies of all the Non-fiction Skills Big Book pages for interactive work (*The Magic Wood* pages 20–21, *How to Get to the Museum* pages 22–23, *Funny-Face Biscuits* pages 24–25 and *Beautiful Bathing* pages 26–27)
- Audio recordings of directories in *The Magic Wood* and *How to Get to the Museum*
- A short video clip of Simon Says
- Interactive word and sentence work for Sessions 2, 3 and 4
- All the Resource Sheets for independent work for you to customise
- Comprehensive Teaching and Planning Guides for the unit are also available on the CD.

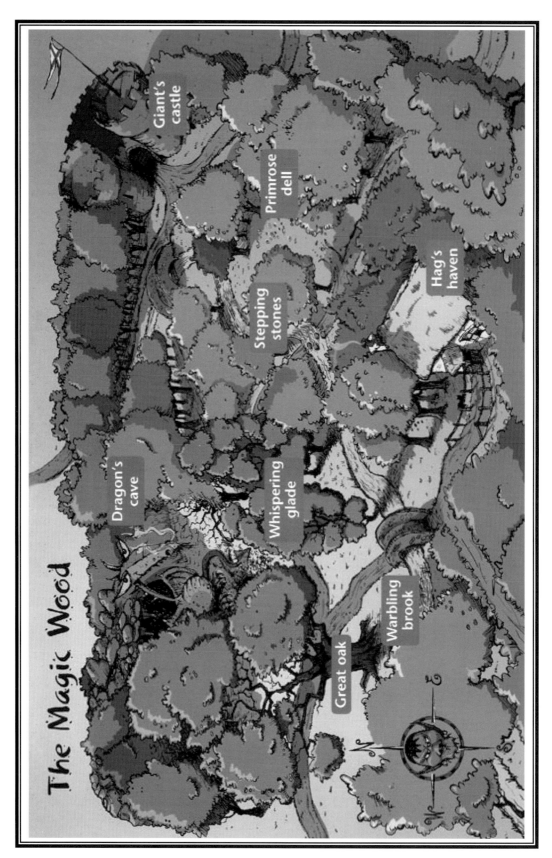

Template for a Twizzer

Materials

Template
Thin cardboard (20cm x 8cm)
Good quality string (70cm)

Equipment

Scissors
Large nail
Glue
Coloured pens
Pencil

Template for a Balancing Bird

You will need:

- Scissors
- 2 x 1p coins or 2 x 2p coins
- card (30cm x 30cm)
- Pencil
- Coloured pens
- Sellotape

How to Play Tiddlywinks

You will need:

A shallow pot or saucer

4 winks (counters) of the same colour per team

1 large squidger (large counter)

A carpeted area to play on

Two rulers

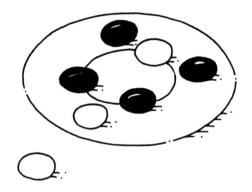

How to play:

_____

_____

_____

_____

_____

_____

_____

_____

_____

_____

_____

_____

_____

_____

_____

_____

RESOURCE **5** SHEET

A Perfect Bath

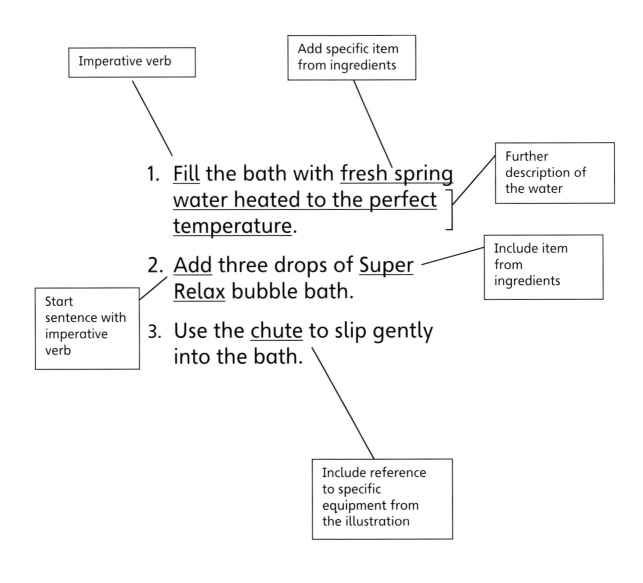

Imperative verb

Add specific item from ingredients

1. Fill the bath with fresh spring water heated to the perfect temperature.

Further description of the water

2. Add three drops of Super Relax bubble bath.

Include item from ingredients

Start sentence with imperative verb

3. Use the chute to slip gently into the bath.

Include reference to specific equipment from the illustration

A Recipe for a Perfect Bath

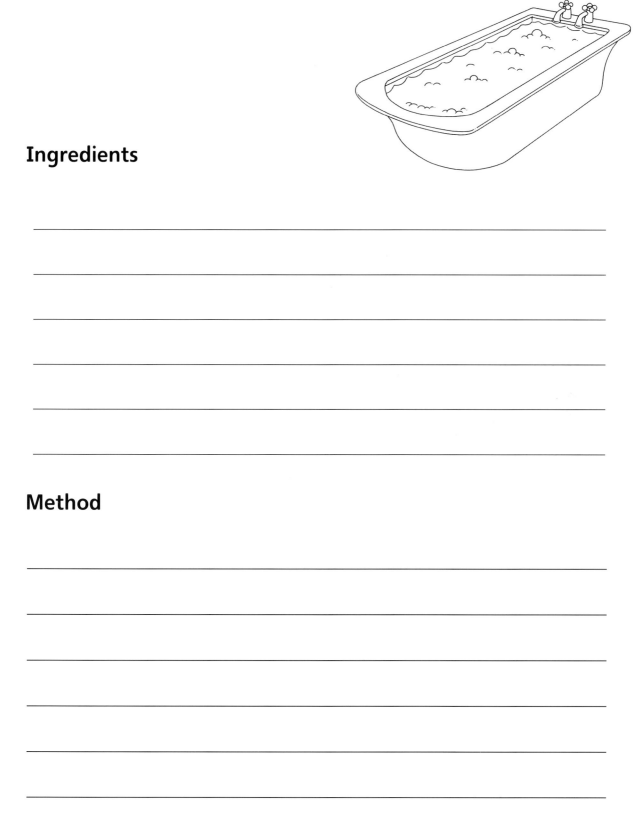

Ingredients

_____

_____

_____

_____

_____

Method

_____

_____

_____

_____

_____

KEY INFORMATION

TEACHING OBJECTIVES

TEXT LEVEL

T2 T17 to make clear notes through, e.g.
- discussing the purpose of note-making and looking at simple examples;
- identifying the purpose for which particular notes will be used;
- identifying key words, phrases or sentences in reading;
- exploring ways of writing in shortened forms, e.g. notes, lists, headlines, telegrams, to understand that some words are more essential to meaning than others;
- making use of simple formats to capture key points, e.g. flow chart, 'for' and 'against' columns, matrices to complete in writing or on screen;
- identifying intended audience, i.e. self or others.

SENTENCE LEVEL

T2 S10 to understand the differences between verbs in the 1st, 2nd and 3rd person...

T2 S11 to understand the need for grammatical agreement in speech and writing...
GfW Unit 14

WORD LEVEL

T2 W19 to use dictionaries to learn or check the spellings and definitions of words

T2 W20 to write their own definitions of words, developing precision and accuracy in expression

T2 W21 to use the term 'definition'

T2 W22 to know the quartiles of the dictionary, e.g. 'm' lies around the half way mark, 't' towards the end.

T2 W23 to organise words or information alphabetically, using the first two letters.

UNIT SUMMARY

RESOURCES

- **Essential Non-fiction Anthology** *The Romans; Roman Sports and Games; Gladiators; Children in Roman Times*
- **Non-fiction Skills Big Book** *From a Dictionary; From a Thesaurus; Making Notes; Roman Food and Drink*
- **Resource Sheets** 1–6
- **Literacy World Interactive** Unit 4

In this flexible two-week unit children learn about the purpose of note making, and make notes in various ways. They practise using dictionaries and create a class dictionary about the Romans.

5–14 GUIDELINES

Reading level B/C
- Reading for information
- Reflecting on the writer's craft
- Knowledge about language

CHILDREN'S TARGETS

READING

I know how to use a dictionary and a thesaurus.

WRITING

I know how and when to write short notes.

SENTENCE

I can identify the 1st, 2nd and 3rd person and I know what sort of texts they are used in.

WORD

I can check spellings or definitions in a dictionary.

SPEAKING AND LISTENING

I can work with a partner and discuss choices.

WIDER CURRICULUM LINKS

Links to: History (The Romans)

●●● *Literacy World* GUIDED READING LINKS

- *A Dictionary of Eponyms* (Core)

OUTLINE PLAN

STAGE **1** TERM **2** UNIT **4**

SESSION	WHOLE CLASS WORK		INDEPENDENT WORK	GUIDED GROUPS	WHOLE CLASS WORK plenary
1 Monday	**Word work** Children investigate the uses of a dictionary, and look at a range of dictionary styles. They review alphabetical order and some dictionary features **W19 W21 W22**		**Independent writing** Make an alphabet of animals **RS1 W23**	**Guided oral work** (support) Revise alphabet order	What targets do we want to achieve in this unit? Brainstorm fun ideas for dictionaries
2 Tuesday (optional)	**Word work** Features of alphabetical texts **W23**	**Shared writing** Demonstrate writing definition of a word. Compare with words on BB dictionary pages **W20 W21**	**Independent writing** Underline key facts and write definitions **RS2**	**Guided Reading** (core) Look up definitions	Children guess whether they are hearing a report text or a definition from a dictionary
3 Wednesday	**Shared reading and word work** Discuss features of thesaurus with reference to BB exemplar. Talk about different meanings of words spelt the same. Look at synonyms and antonyms **W16**		**Independent writing** Children practise accurate use of synonyms using **RS3 W17**	**Guided reading** (core) Using a thesaurus	Class think up antonyms and synonyms
4 Thursday (optional)	**Shared reading** Read Anthology information about Romans. Demonstrate identifying key ideas. Tell them these form basis of notes	**Sentence work** Look at pronouns in first, second and third person **S10 S11** *(GfW14)*	**Independent writing** Make notes about Romans from Anthology text **T17**	**Guided writing** (support) Make notes	Discuss notes from independent work
5 Friday	**Shared reading and note-making** Demonstrate note making by deleting extra words **T17**	**Sentence work** Look at verb tenses **S10 S11** *(GfW14)*	**Independent writing** Practise deleting non-essential words using **RS4**	**Guided writing** (support) Use **RS4** to help group to identify essential text	Individuals share notes made in independent work and the others turn them back into sentences
6 Monday	**Shared reading and writing** Teacher demo recording information from Anthology on a spidergram. **T17**		**Independent writing** Make notes using a spidergram	**Guided writing** (support) Group add to spidergram	Introduce next area of research and find information in a video clip
7 Tuesday (optional)	**Shared reading and writing** Demonstrate how to label diagram of gladiator using information from Anthology **T17**		**Independent writing** Draw and label Retiarius	**Guided reading** (extension) Research Roman armour	Extension group share their findings and class add them in labels to Big Book
8 Wednesday (optional)	**Shared writing** Demonstrate how to list information in 2 columns. Distribute text for class to extract information **RS6**	**Sentence work** Practise changing first to third person using **RS5**	**Independent writing** Choose format for notes and collect information about subject	**Guided Reading** (core) Support group to make notes of information on Internet or CD-ROM **T17**	We can arrange our subjects into alphabetical order.
9 Thursday	**Shared writing** Remind class about different forms of note-making. Demonstrate how to make a dictionary entry **W20**	**Extended independent writing** Class to compose paragraphs changing notes into complete sentences **W20**		**Guided writing** (extension) Review research and support group to select key information	Class revise completed entries and discuss limitations of dictionaries as research tools
10 Friday (optional)	**Shared writing** Class arrange their work in alphabetical order in scrap-book. Discuss what they have learned about making notes		**Independent writing** Refine dictionary entries	**Guided writing** (core) Refine dictionary entry	Play a quiz game and a dictionary race. Reflect on unit targets and the work done

Abbreviation key
GfW Grammar for Writing
SpB Spelling Bank
RS Resource Sheet

TEACHING NOTES

SESSION (1)

FOCUS

- **What is the purpose of a dictionary?**
- **How are dictionaries organised?**

RESOURCES

- Resource Sheet 1 *Animal Alphabet*
- Set of Alphabet cards
- Copies of the class dictionary

WORD WORK

Introduce the unit and share the targets. Explain that in this unit they will be learning how to use a dictionary and to make notes. They will make a class dictionary about the Romans.

Ask the class what a dictionary is and when we use one. Do they know how a dictionary is organised? Introduce the dictionary activities for this session.

Alphabetical order: Write the alphabet on the board and sing an alphabet song. Point at a letter and then at a child and ask them to say the name of the next letter in the alphabet.

Which letter is the most common? Tell the children to work with a partner. First they guess which letter has the most entries (number of pages) and which has the fewest, writing their predictions on their whiteboards. Then they check in their dictionaries (*'c' and 's' have the most; 'x' and 'z' are the least*). *Quartiles:* Ask the children to predict which letter will occur in the middle of the dictionary *(m)* Explain the four quartiles of the dictionary approximately a–d; e–m; n–r; s–z. Choose a word and challenge the children to open the dictionary at that word. Who is at the right letter? Who is nearest to the word?

Sorting names alphabetically: Ask the girls to come out and line up in alphabetical order according to their first name. What will they do if two girls have names starting with the same letter? Talk about second letter order. Ask the boys to check that the line-up is accurate, then come out and line up in alphabetical order according to their surnames.

Sorting words alphabetically: Write the following words on the board: *mouse, lion, map, nut.* Ask the children to write them in alphabetical order on their whiteboards. Do the same with *clock, blue, dog, brush.* Talk about the words that start with the same letter – how are they sorted?

INDEPENDENT WRITING

Give each pair of children a copy of RS1. They are to devise an 'animal alphabet', using the dictionary to help them.

↪ **Extension** challenge children to think of other animals that they could have chosen for each letter and list them in alphabetical order.

GUIDED ORAL WORK — SUPPORT

Check the group are all familiar with the alphabet letter names. Can they say the alphabet? Play alphabet order games using a set of alphabet cards (e.g. *What's missing?* (remove a card from a sequence of 6); *What's next?* (put down 3 letters in sequence and ask them to put down the next three)). Reinforce the process of using a dictionary to find words by monitoring and supporting them as they look them up.

PLENARY

Brainstorm any titles of dictionaries that would be fun to have around. (e.g. *a dictionary of football terms; a dictionary of computer games; a dictionary of cartoon characters*). Brainstorm other texts that are organised in alphabetical order (e.g. *directories*). Ask the children why they think they are organised in this way. Tell them to look around at home and to find one example of a text that is organised in alphabetical order (or with an index).

SESSION (2) OPTIONAL

FOCUS

- **What are the features of a dictionary?**

RESOURCES

- Non-fiction Skills Big Book page 28 *From a Dictionary*
- Resource Sheet 2 *Creating Definitions from Descriptions*
- Class dictionaries (individual or one between two)

WORD WORK

Ask the children about any alphabetical texts they found at home. List them and add to the list during the unit as children come across other texts.

Show them Big Book p.28 and point out the features of a dictionary (*alphabetical order; head word; guide word; definition: in note form, exemplar sentence, word class, plural or singular, verb tense and pronunciation guide; use of colour and occasional illustration*). Make a list of these features to refer to later. Talk about how each feature helps the reader find the information required.

💬 **Time out for discussion** Tell the children to work with a partner and to look at a class dictionary to see how many features it has in common with the dictionary text in the Big Book. Are there any additional features (e.g. *word origin*)?

Provide some practice in using the features by asking children to answer specific questions, modified to fit the features of the class dictionary (e.g. *Look for the word 'long'. Which 2 word classes does it belong to? Can you give examples of each?*)

SHARED WRITING

Demonstration writing Explain to the class that you are going to write a dictionary definition for the word 'dog'. Write the word on the board and then add some complete sentences (e.g. *A dog is a four legged animal. All dogs have tails. Dogs make good pets but some dogs bark if they are left alone at home*).

Ask the children if you have written a good definition. Does it include the important details about a dog? Are there any bits that are not needed in a definition? Underline the essential facts: *four-legged animal, pets, bark.*

Compare your entry with an example in the Big Book. What do the children notice is different? *(e.g. not in full sentences, do not include personal opinion)*. Rewrite the definition along the lines of the Big Book entries *(e.g. Dog: a four-legged animal that barks. Dogs are often kept as pets)*.

Ready, steady, write Ask the children to write a definition of the word 'cat' in the same style. Remind them to stick to essential facts, avoid pesonal opinions and write in note form.

INDEPENDENT WRITING

Give each child a copy of RS2. These are descriptions, not definitions. Tell them to underline the key facts and then write the definitions. Ask two children to prepare their definitions for use in the plenary.

Support Read the descriptions with the support group and help them to identify the key information to be underlined on RS2.

GUIDED READING — CORE

Use the class dictionaries to look up the definitions of a selection of words. Check the children's ability to use the features of the dictionary to help them search effectively. Talk about ways to find information quickly. Challenge the children to find words 'against the clock'. Explore the dictionary further and talk about its uses *(e.g. special word lists at the back)*.

PLENARY

Examine the definitions prepared for discussion and ask the children to compare their versions. Do they sound like dictionary definitions?

Tell the children you are going to read to them either a dictionary text or another non-fiction book. The children are to determine which is which *(e.g. Dinosaur: a large pre-historic reptile./Dinosaurs lived many thousands of years ago; Many people enjoy riding horses./Horse: a large mammal with a mane and a tail)*.

What features indicate that a text is from a dictionary? Compare to the list of features made earlier.

SESSION 3

FOCUS

● **What is a thesaurus?**

RESOURCES

● Non-fiction Skills Big Book page 29 *From a Thesaurus*
● Resource Sheet 3 *Synonyms*
● Make 15 small cards saying 'Funny – Ha Ha!' and 15 saying 'Funny peculiar'

SHARED READING AND WORD WORK

Limbering up Ask the children to decide which definition of a thesaurus is correct: *a prehistoric animal; a disease; a reference book with words of similar meanings listed together*. Show them examples of thesauruses.

Look at Big Book p.29 and explain the difference between a dictionary and a thesaurus. Look at the thesaurus entries for 'full'. Talk about choosing the best word based on the context. Ask the class when it might be helpful to use a thesaurus.

Time out for thinking Talk about the difference between 'funny' meaning a joke (Ha! Ha!) and 'funny' meaning 'odd' (Peculiar). Give each pair a set of the cards (*see* Resources). Read some thesaurus entries for 'funny' for the children to identify by holding up a card.

Write the following sentences on the board: *The player dropped to the ground. The boy was dropped from the team. The school dropped the plan to build a swimming pool.* Tell the children to work with a partner to find a synonym for each use of the verb 'dropped'.

Share their answers and generate as many synonyms for each use of the word as possible. Demonstrate how to use a thesaurus to look for synonyms.

INDEPENDENT WRITING

Give each child a copy of RS3 and ask them to identify the accurate use of each synonym.

Extension Give the children 2 minutes to list as many synonyms as they can for the word 'sad', then use a thesaurus to find even more. Working in pairs, they compose sentences that show the precise meanings.

GUIDED READING — CORE

Provide copies of a thesaurus. Skim through together and identify specific features. Use the thesaurus to explore particular words and monitor their ability to use it effectively. Discuss the difference between dictionaries and thesauruses.

PLENARY

Talk about the idea of expressing shades of meaning in the context of the extension group's words for 'sad'.

Remind the class that many thesauruses provide opposites (*antonyms*) as well as synonyms. Write the following words on the board and challenge the children to think of opposites and then to think of synonyms for the opposites (e.g. large (*small, tiny, minute*) kind, new, lively).

SESSION (4) OPTIONAL

FOCUS

- **How do you identify the key idea in a paragraph?**

RESOURCES

- Non-fiction Skills Big Book p.30–31 *Making Notes*
- Essential Non-fiction Anthology pages 28–29 *The Romans*

SHARED READING

? Limbering up Tell the children to turn to a partner and to spend two minutes thinking of anything they know about the Romans. Collect in the children's suggestions on to the board. Then group any linked ideas into a spidergram *(information about soldiers, gladiators, etc.)* Ask the children what headings they could give to each group. Write these on the board *(e.g. family life, slaves, army, buildings and roads)*. Explain that, throughout the rest of the unit, they will read a variety of information about the Romans, make notes and then use it to compile a dictionary.

Read to the class the background information about the Romans in the Anthology pp.28–29. Check this information against any ideas on the board.

Ask the children what is different about the information on the board and the information in the Anthology *(one is in the style of a report text, the other is in brief note form; one is in sentences and one is not)*.

Look again at the first paragraph about the Romans on p.28. Ask the children to identify the key ideas in the paragraph *(called Romans – lived in Italy)*. Underline key words or phrases using the acetate sheet. How is your note different from the first sentence? *(not a full sentence, shorter, only gives essential information e.g. does not explain that they were a small tribe called the Latins)*.

Look at the notes in the Big Book pp.30–31 for the paragraph 'The Roman Empire'. Ask the children what information has been left out of the notes? *(No mention of gods, nor that soldiers were well paid, etc)*. Explain that these are interesting facts but they are not essential: notes just pick out the essential information.

💬 **Time out for discussion** Tell the children to work with a partner, find the main idea in paragraph 2, and write it in note form on their whiteboards. Compare their answers with the notes in the Big Book p.31.

SENTENCE WORK

Talk about pronouns in the 1st, 2nd or 3rd person *(I or we; you; he, she, it or they)*. Select examples of texts written in each, read short extracts and ask children to identify the pronouns. Explain the idea of 1st or 3rd person. Reread texts and ask children to identify the person. Check their answers and talk about what is typical of particular types of text. *(Links with GfW Unit 4.)*

INDEPENDENT WORK

Ask the children to work with a partner and to make notes from the paragraphs 'The Romans in Britain' and 'Life under Roman rule' in the Anthology pp.28–29. Remind them to make the notes under the relevant paragraph headings and to write just the main ideas, not full sentences.

GUIDED WRITING — SUPPORT

Write some simple sentences about the school day (talk about punctuation and spelling as you demonstrate). Tell the children you are going to reduce a sentence to a short note. Ask them which are the important words. Underline these and then write a note form of the sentence. Read a second sentence and ask a child to underline the important words. Then ask the children in pairs to reduce the sentence to a short note. Do the same with the other sentences reminding the children that the note contains the key information and that it is not punctuated like a full sentence.

PLENARY

Discuss the notes the children have made in independent work. Compare them with the notes on Big Book on p.31.

SESSION (5)

FOCUS

- **When do you use notes?**

RESOURCES

- Non-fiction Skills Big Book pages 30–31 *Making Notes*; pages 32–33 *Roman Food and Drink*
- Essential Non-fiction Anthology pages 28–29 *The Romans*
- Resource Sheet 4 *Roman Roads*

SHARED READING AND NOTE-MAKING

? Limbering up Tell the children to turn to a partner and to think of occasions when we write notes. Share these ideas *(e.g. notes to another teacher, notes by the phone, reminder notes, notes to other members of the family)*.

Look at 'Top tips for taking notes' on Big Book p.31. Can the children think of any other good ideas to remember when note-making? *(abbreviate some words, e.g. bk for book; writing some words in red to stand out)*. Explain to the children that we often organise notes in the form of a diagram, such as a spidergram.

Demonstration writing Read the Big Book text on pp.32–33 *Roman Food and Drink*. Explain that one way to identify the key information for notes is to cross out the non-essential words. Using the acetate sheet demonstrate this on paragraph 1. Explain that 'notes' are what is left after the deletions.

Teacher scribing Ask the children to suggest which words to delete on p.33.

SENTENCE WORK

When we use the pronouns 'I' and 'We' we are using the 1st person; 'you' is the 2nd person and 'he' 'she' 'it' and 'they' are the 3rd person. Explain that the text is in the 3rd person. Make up some sentences for the children to identify which person is being used. Explain that the verb in the sentence must match the pronoun. Write the sentence *I like swimming.* (first person) Then write *He _____ swimming.* Ask the children to jot down the verb on their whiteboards (*likes*). Explain that the 'being' verb to follow 'we' is 'were'. This is easy to remember because they both start with 'we'. Ask children to write on their whiteboards *We were singing. We were happy. We were working.* (Links with GfW Unit 14.)

INDEPENDENT WRITING

Give each child a copy of RS4. Tell them to delete the non-essential words and then put the remaining information in note form under the headings.

GUIDED WRITING — SUPPORT

Read the text on RS4 to the group. Work through it sentence by sentence deciding which text is essential and which is less important. Ask the children to cross out the less important text. Then help them to connect the words that have not been crossed out into notes under the headings supplied.

PLENARY

Ask individual children to read out their notes for a paragraph. Discuss with the class whether these are the same points they had identified. Explain that you are going to use their notes and reconstruct the information as whole sentences. Demonstrate this, talking through your decisions as you do so. Continue in the same way for the remaining paragraphs.

SESSION 6

FOCUS

● **How does a spidergram help to organise information?**

RESOURCES

● Essential Non-fiction Anthology pages 30–31 *Roman Sports and Games*
● A video clip of gladiators from, e.g. *Gladiator, Spartacus, Ben Hur* (optional)

SHARED READING AND WRITING

Read the information about Roman sports and games in the Anthology on pp.30–31.

Ask them questions based on the information, such as:

What was the favourite pastime of rich Roman men? What games did they play? Why was chariot racing so dangerous? etc.

Teacher demonstration Tell the children that you are going to make notes about this spread in the form of a spidergram. Draw an outline of a spidergram on the board.

Time out for discussion Give the children one minute to agree with a partner what the heading in the centre oval should be? (*Roman sports and games*) Ask the children to look back at the Anthology text and to decide how many 'legs' the spidergram is going to need (*5 – one for each heading*).

Demonstrate how to present the information from the first paragraph in the first leg of the spidergram (*Roman baths: favourite pastime; daily; hot and cold baths*).

Teacher scribing Ask the children to suggest where to put 'Friendly games' and 'Public games'.

Supported composition Tell the children to work with a partner and to write on their whiteboards *Fights at the Colosseum.* Take in their suggestions and discuss them with the class and add the information to the class spidergram.

INDEPENDENT WRITING

Tell the children to work with a partner and to read the information about 'A Day at the Races'. They should draw a spidergram with four legs and note the information on it.

GUIDED WRITING — SUPPORT

Read 'A Day at the Races' to the group. Talk through the information to ensure the children understand the content. Sketch a spidergram with four legs and ask the children which notes should go by each 'leg'. Write their suggestions. Discuss spellings as you write.

PLENARY

Introduce the next area of research – gladiators. Show the class a clip from a video e.g. *Ben Hur, Gladiator* or *Spartacus.* Note 3 more things you have learnt from it about gladiators.

SESSION 7 OPTIONAL

FOCUS

● **How do you write a label?**

RESOURCES

● Non-fiction Skills Big Book pages 34–35 *Illustrations of Gladiators*
● Essential Non-fiction Anthology pages 32–33 *Roman Gladiators*

SHARED READING AND WRITING

Read the information about Gladiators on pp.32–33 of the Anthology, and check they have understood it.

Limbering up What is a label and when are they used? Explain that labelling a diagram is another way of noting the essential information from a text.

Teacher scribing Show the class the gladiators on pp.34–35 of the Big Book. Ask them to read about the Samnite and to decide which he is. Discuss the features of labels (*no capital letters; print rather than joined script; arrows*). Label his amour and weapons on the acetate sheet. Do the same with the Thracian and Murmillo.

INDEPENDENT WRITING

Ask the children to draw their own picture of Retiarius, based on Anthology p.33. Tell them to reread the paragraph in the Anthology and label their drawings.

GUIDED READING — EXTENSION

Give the group a selection of books about the Romans and ask them to find out the accurate names for some of the armour worn by the gladiators (*e.g. different kinds of shields, visors, daggers, swords, leg-guards*).

PLENARY

Ask the extension group to share their findings and add these technical names to the labels in the Big Book. Talk about the process of presenting information in the form of a labelled diagram – has this helped them to remember what they were reading about? How did they select the most important information?

SESSION 8 OPTIONAL

FOCUS

- **Why might you display information in a chart?**

RESOURCES

- Essential Non-fiction Anthology pages 34–35 *Children in Roman Times*
- Resource Sheet 5 *Dictionary Entries*
- Resource Sheet 6 *By a Roman Child*
- Library books on the Romans
- Access to the Internet

SHARED READING WRITING

Read the Anthology pp.34–35 and talk about the information about boys and girls in Roman times.

Teacher scribing Tell the children that another way of presenting notes is in a chart and that you are going to display the information about Roman children in a chart in two columns: *Differences in the Lives of Boys and Girls in Roman Times*. Draw the columns and headings on the board. Reread the first paragraph and ask the children what brief information should go in each column (*Boys: grow up to have much power; Girls: some given away*). Look at paragraph 2 and add the information about the different lifestyles. Complete the chart and discuss the differences. Would it be better to be a boy or a girl in Roman times?

SENTENCE WORK

Read the text on RS6 as the children follow. Identify the person it is written in and talk about changing it to the third person. Which words will need to be changed? Involve the children in making changes and checking for subject–verb agreement.

Planning Cut up RS5 and allocate one card to each child (see suggestions for support and extension groups below). Explain that they going to write a class 'Dictionary of Rome and the Romans'. The children will write a definition of the topic on their chosen card. They will need to collect together the information for their entry from the work they have done already and to do some further research. They can use the Anthology, other library books and the Internet. (*Links with GfW Unit 14.*)

INDEPENDENT WRITING

Each child starts looking for information about their subject – have they already read about it and made notes? Do they need to read more? Encourage them to use strategies they have learnt during the unit.

- **Support** Give the children needing support cards relating to the source material read earlier in this session (*e.g. babies, girls, boys, education, children's games, children's clothes*). If possible, provide additional reference material for them to use as a group.
- **Extension** Give pairs of children the following cards: *army, empire, roads*. Challenge them to devise their own 'mini-dictionaries' by defining the main word and a series of other related words.

GUIDED READING — CORE

Talk about ways of researching the words on their cards. Support the children in using the Internet or a CD-ROM encyclopedia and in making relevant and succinct notes.

PLENARY

Explain that the dictionary entries will need to be organised in alphabetical order. Holding their subject cards, the children arrange themselves into alphabetical order. Make a note of the order and record it for future reference.

SESSION 9

FOCUS

- **How do you write definitions?**

RESOURCES

- Essential Non-fiction Anthology pages 34–35 *Children in Roman Times*
- Resource Sheet 6 *Dictionary Entries*
- Library books on the Romans
- Access to the Internet

SHARED WRITING

Talk for writing Remind the children that they have been researching specific information for the class dictionary, which is meant to be a source of quick facts about aspects of Roman life. The entries should be short and accurate, not long reports.

Demonstration writing Show the children how to use notes on one subject, to compose a dictionary entry in complete sentences. Emphasise that this will be just one paragraph containing some essential facts, but not everything there is to say on the subject.

Discuss expanding the definition by adding a map or labelled diagram.

EXTENDED INDEPENDENT WRITING

Ask the children to review their notes and identify the most important information (*e.g. by highlighting*). They can then go on to compose their paragraph in complete sentences. Remind them to read through their writing and check it for factual accuracy, spelling and punctuation.

➤ **Extension** Children can go on expand their entry with an illustration, map or labelled diagram.

GUIDED WRITING EXTENSION

Review the research done by each pair of children. What other subjects are related to their word? (*e.g. empire: emperors, expansion, decline; army: legions, centurions, weapons; roads: construction, location, surviving roads*). Support them in selecting relevant information from their notes. Monitor their ability to compose complete sentences based on factual information. Discuss illustrations.

PLENARY

Review some completed entries. Talk about the purpose of the dictionary and its limitations (*i.e. useful for finding out information quickly but no good for detailed research*). Using the shared writing, demonstrate how to add a final sentence giving details of how to find out more (*e.g. the title and author of a useful reference book, a website*).

SESSION (10) OPTIONAL

FOCUS

- **What have you learned about dictionaries and note making?**

RESOURCES

- Scrap book

SHARED WRITING

Before the Session, prepare a scrap book (or sugar paper book) with headings on each page, using the headwords listed alphabetically in Session 8.

Teacher scribing Show the children the book and put in the shared writing text on 'Rome'. Discuss the title and ask children for suggestions for an introductory paragraph about how to use the book. Collect their ideas and involve them in suggesting how to make notes to record the best suggestions. Turn the notes into a few sentences explaining what the dictionary is for and how to use it.

INDEPENDENT WRITING

Give the children time to review their completed dictionary entries and make changes as necessary. Have they added details of where the reader can find out more? Have they included any illustrations?

GUIDED WRITING CORE

Support the children in reviewing their dictionary entries. Have they included the most important facts? Have they written consistently in the third person? Monitor their ability to check and correct their work.

PLENARY: EVALUATION AND REVIEW

Stick each piece of paper into the scrap book (or a homemade sugar paper book) – one per page. Demonstrate how to use the book and read some of the definitions. Talk about how the book could be used.

Prepare two activities to help the children consolidate what they have learnt during this unit: a Dictionary race and a Romans quiz.

1. Give the children a dictionary each. Read out a series of words for them to define. Who can find them first? What strategies do they use?

2. Have a quick quiz on what the children have learned about the Romans.

   - *Which Emperor built the wall in England near the Scottish border?*
   - *What did 'thumbs up' in the Colosseum mean?*
   - *What were children given to wear around their necks when they were one week old?*
   - *Which of the gladiators had a net?*
   - *Why were the roads built with a curved top?*
   - *Who fought in the Colosseum?*
   - *Who did the work in the homes of wealthy Romans?*
   - *What happened to sickly babies?*

Revisit the unit targets. Talk about evidence of the children's progress looking at the class dictionary and other work they have done during the unit.

Literacy World

INTERACTIVE CD

On the Literacy World Interactive CD for Stage 1 Non-fiction, you will find the following resources for this unit:

- Copies of all the Non-fiction Skills Big Book pages for this unit for interactive work (*From a Dictionary* page 28, *From a Thesaurus* page 29, *Making Notes* pages 30–31, *Roman Food and Drink* pages 32–33 and *Gladiators* pages 34–35)
- Short video clips about Gladiators and Roman food
- Interactive word and sentence work for Session 1
- All the Resource Sheets for independent work for you to customise
- Comprehensive Teaching and Planning Guides for the unit are also available on the CD.

Name _____   Date _____

Animal Alphabet

a. _____   n. _____

b. _____   o. _____

c. _____   p. _____

d. _____   q. quail

e. _____   r. _____

f. _____   s. _____

g. _____   t. _____

h. _____   u. _____

i. _____   v. _____

j. _____   w. _____

k. _____   x. x-ray fish

l. _____   y. yak

m. _____   z. _____

Literacy World

STAGE 1 | TERM 2 | For use with Unit 4 Session 1: Independent work

© Harcourt Education Ltd. 2004. Copying permitted for purchasing school only. The material is not copyright free.

Creating Definitions from Descriptions

Underline the important information in each description. Then write a brief definition using only the important facts. (Remember to leave out any personal opinions.)

Description: Trees
Trees are beautiful and they are the largest plants on earth. Each tree has a trunk from which branches grow. Trees which have low branches are easier to climb. On the branches there are leaves. I like trees in the winter best when they have lost their leaves.

Definition: Tree

_____

_____

Description: Cars
Cars are vehicles with an engine. Most have four wheels but some have three. Cars are quite small and only about four or five people can usually fit in a car. My car is quite old but I will get a new one next year.

Definition: Car

_____

_____

Description: Rabbits
Rabbits are cute and cuddly and make very good pets. They are four-legged, furry mammals. Rabbits have long ears and a short tail and they like being stroked. They eat grass, oats and grain. If they get the chance they will eat the flowers in your garden.

Definition: Rabbit

_____

_____

Synonyms

Read the synonyms for the following words:

Drink:	sip	gulp	lap
Eat:	bolt	nibble	feast
Cut:	fell	shave	mow
Clean:	blank	polished	pure

Choose the correct word to match each definition.

1. to drink with the tongue like a cat _____
2. to drink a small amount at a time _____
3. to drink greedily _____

4. to eat a little bit at a time _____
5. to eat very quickly _____
6. to eat a very grand meal _____

7. to cut down a tree _____
8. to cut hair from a man's face _____
9. to cut grass _____

10. a clean piece of paper _____
11. a clean car _____
12. clean water _____

Roman Roads

Read the information about Romans and their roads. Cross out all the unimportant words and write this essential information as notes.

Roman roads
Romans are famous for their long, straight roads. They built them all over their Empire. Good roads meant their army could move quickly from one place to another.

The straight Roman roads
In England, before the Romans invaded, roads were dusty winding paths which went round the edges of fields or around hills. The Roman roads took the shortest, straightest route through fields and over hills.

How the Romans built their roads
Romans built roads of stone. First they dug a trench and filled it with layers of large stones. Then they put a layer of smaller stones on top. Above that they put gravel which they rammed down. On the surface they used stone slabs. The top layer of stones was curved slightly so that rainwater would run off the surface.

Roman roads today
There are still routes of old Roman roads in England today. The A1 (M) which runs from London to York was originally the Roman road called Ermine Street.

Roman roads

- _____

- _____

The straight Roman roads

- _____

- _____

How the Romans built their roads

- _____

- _____

Dictionary Entries

Empire	Thracian
Roads	Retiarius
Army	Slaves
Hannibal	Latin
Hadrian	Marriage
Feasts	Houses
Food – poor	Babies
Food – wealthy	Girls
Colosseum	Boys
Friendly games	Education
Baths	Children's games
Circus Maximus	Children's clothes
Samnite	Murmillo

STAGE 1 | TERM 2 | For use with Unit 4 Sessions 8 and 9: Independent work
© Harcourt Education Ltd. 2004. Copying permitted for purchasing school only. The material is not copyright free.

By a Roman Child

My name is name is Marcus and I am 10 years old. I live in a villa near the great city of Rome. My father is a merchant and we are quite rich. I have an older brother who is 14 and a younger sister who is 8. My sister and I both wear short tunics but my brother has just started to wear grown-up clothes. He no longer has any lessons because he is working with my father. I have a teacher at home who teaches me how to read, write and add up. My sister does not have lessons with me, but my mother teaches her how to spin and weave cloth and she will learn how to run a household when she is older.

My favourite game is marbles which I play with the slave boys in our household. Once we went to see a chariot race at the Circus Maximus – it was the most exciting thing I have ever seen.

1 3 5 Writing Letters

KEY INFORMATION

TEACHING OBJECTIVES

TEXT LEVEL

T3 T16 to read examples of letters written for a range of purposes

T3 T19 to summarise orally in one sentence the content of a passage or text and the main point it is making

T3 T20 to write letters, notes and messages linked to work in other subjects … selecting style and vocabulary appropriate to the intended reader

T3 T21 to use IT to bring to a published form

T3 T22 experiment with recounting the same event in a variety of ways

T3 T23 to organise letters into simple paragraphs

T3 T26 to summarise in writing the content of a passage or text and the main point it is making

SENTENCE LEVEL

T3 S1 to use awareness of grammar to decipher new or unfamiliar words

T3 S3 to ensure grammatical agreement in speech and writing of pronouns and verbs

T3 S6 to investigate through reading and writing how words and phrases can signal time sequences
GfW Unit 18

WORD LEVEL

T3 W1 to revise the spelling of words containing each of the long vowel phonemes

T3 W6 to use independent spelling strategies

T3 W7 to practise new spellings regularly by 'Look, Say, Cover, Write, Check'

UNIT SUMMARY

RESOURCES

- **Essential Non-fiction Anthology** *Letters: Recount, Complaint, Explanation, Congratulation; Uplands Farm Brochure; Kinds of Letters*
- **Non-fiction Skills Big Book** *Sending Messages; Letter of Enquiry; Formal Letter*
- **Resource Sheets** 1–8
- **Literacy World Interactive** Unit 5

In this two-week unit children read a selection of different types of letter varying in purpose and degree of formality. They learn about the layout and language features of different letters and produce formal and informal letters linked to the theme of the farm.

5–14 GUIDELINES

Reading level B/C
- Reflecting on the writer's craft
- Awareness of genre
- Knowledge about language

CHILDREN'S TARGETS

READING
I know the difference between formal and informal letters.

WRITING
I can write letters in a variety of styles.

SENTENCE
I can use sentence starters like 'First, Next, Then, Later'.

WORD
I know how to learn to spell tricky words.

SPEAKING AND LISTENING
I can take part in a class discussion.

WIDER CURRICULUM LINKS

Citizenship: taking part – developing skills of communication and participation.

GUIDED READING LINKS

- *How a Book is Made* (Core and Satellites)

OUTLINE PLAN

SESSION	WHOLE CLASS WORK		INDEPENDENT WORK	GUIDED GROUPS	WHOLE CLASS WORK plenary
1 Monday	**Oral language work** Bring in sample letters. Ask the class why people write letters and if they have written any themselves **T16 T19**	**Sentence work** Look at words that signal time sequence. Demonstrate how to improve sentences **S6**	**Independent writing** Join sentences with connectives using **RS1**	**Guided reading** (core) Look at style and purpose of different letters	What targets do we hope to achieve in this unit. Start a class list of connectives
2 Tuesday	**Shared reading and writing** Discuss language of persuasion in context of the farm brochure in the Anthology. Look at the features of a postcard on BB page 36. Model writing postcard using BB frame **T20**		**Independent writing** Write a postcard on **RS2** **T20**	**Guided writing** (support) Rehearse sentences for postcard aloud before writing them down	Practise writing and decoding terse text messages
3 Wednesday	**Shared reading** Read the recount letter in the Anthology and model writing address **T23**	**Word work** Look at spellings linked to time. Discuss ways of remembering spellings **W6**	**Independent writing** Write account of outing using connectives	**Guided writing** (support) Orally recount a visit to a farm noticing time connectives	Discuss recounts. Look at connectives and add to class list
4 Thursday	**Shared Writing** Demo writing a recount with reference to features on **RS3**. Look at words linking events to time. Discuss planning own recounts **T20**	**Word work** Look at spellings linked to time **W6 W7**	**Independent writing** Write own recount ensuring inclusion of report features	**Guided writing** (core) Discuss features of recounts	Swap recounts and look for linking words. Identify best sentences
5 Friday	**Shared reading and writing** Read the BB letter of enquiry to the class, identify typical features. Demo writing answer on BB writing frame **T16**		**Independent writing** Children write a reply to enquiry using **RS4** **T23 T26**	**Guided Writing** (extension) Group compose complete letter of enquiry	Review different types of letters, looking at typical features
6 Monday	**Shared reading** Discuss features of formal letter writing using BB page 40 as an exemplar **T20**	**Sentence work** Use context to determine the meaning of words **S1**	**Independent work** Complete cloze passage of formal language vocabulary on **RS6**	**Guided writing** (core) Formulate reply to BB letter	Check cloze work, discuss meaning of formal vocabulary and share guided letter
7 Tuesday	**Shared writing** Discuss formal letters and model reply using **RS6** **T20**	**Sentence work** Look at agreement between pronouns and verbs **S3**	**Independent writing** Complete **RS7** (subject and verb agreement)	**Guided writing** (extension) Discuss letter of reply from farmer	Using cards from **RS8**, add pronouns to verbs to make sentences
8 Wednesday	**Shared reading and writing** Brainstorm why people write letters of complaint. Read Anthology example and scribe reply **T20**		**Independent writing** List complaints in Anthology example and suggest replies	**Guided reading** (support) Discuss audience and purpose of formal letters **T23**	Divide class into farmers and ramblers – discuss ways of solving the conflict
9 Thursday	**Shared reading** Examine letters of information and congratulation in the Anthology for formal characteristics. Briefly discuss kinds of letters encountered so far.		**Independent writing** Children play the 'Letter Game' and devise messages in a chosen format between characters on page 43 of the Anthology **T21**	**Guided writing** (core) Rehearse openings and endings of different kinds of letters	Quiz the class about formal and informal features of letters using BB examples. Discuss appropriate language for formal letters
10 Friday	**Shared reading and writing** Discuss writing competition letter extolling Uplands Farm holidays. Demo writing address and signing off **T20**	**Extended independent writing** Write the letter discussed in the shared session		**Guided writing** (support) Rehearse paragraphs for a letter about their stay in the farm What have we	achieved? What could we do better?

TEACHING NOTES

SESSION ①

FOCUS

● **Why do people write letters?**

RESOURCES

● Resource Sheet 1 *Linking Sentences*
● Examples of letters (bills, personal letters, postcards etc.)
● *The Jolly Postman* by Allan Ahlberg

ORAL LANGUAGE WORK

Introduce the unit by telling the children that they will be finding out about different kinds of letters people write for different purposes.

? Limbering up Show the class your selection of letters. Discuss the envelope, stamp and address. Ask them why people write letters. Collect in their ideas and start a class collection of different types of letters. Read snippets of your letters and talk about those which are formal and which are informal. Talk about different ways of addressing the person – Sir, Mr Jones, Joseph, Joe. Which is appropriate for an informal letter and which for a formal?

SENTENCE WORK

Write the following sentence on the board: *I went to a farm and I saw some hens, and then I saw two dogs and then I saw the cows and then I had my tea.*

Ask the children what they think of the sentence, and underline the 'and thens'. Discuss ways to improve the sentences. Write the following on the board: *I saw two dogs and then I looked at the cows.* Ask the children which words link the two clauses (*and then*). Demonstrate other ways of linking the clauses using time sequence words (*e.g. I saw two dogs. Then I saw the cows/After I saw two dogs I looked at the cows/I saw two dogs. After that, I looked at the cows*).

💬 Time out for discussion Write the following sentence on the board: *I fed the hens and then I fed the ducks.* Ask the children to work with a partner to find three ways to link these clauses without using 'and then'.

Collect in the children's suggestions and write them on the board. Talk about how we sometimes link sentences leaving out 'then' and 'I' (*e.g. I fed the cat and then I fed the budgie* could become '*I fed the cat and the budgie.*')

(Links with GfW Unit 18.)

INDEPENDENT WRITING

Tell the children to complete RS1.

↩ Support Write out the passage as a series of sentence strips and provide the connectives on word cards. Ask the children to work in pairs, read the sentences and decide where the linking words could go. They can then write out their new version of the passage.

GUIDED READING — CORE

Share a selection of letters with the group. Talk about the different styles and purposes of the letters. *The Jolly Postman* by Allan Ahlberg has letters suitable for this age group.

PLENARY

Introduce the targets for the unit and talk through what they are going to be doing in order to achieve them.

Look back at connectives that children have encountered in the session, and tell them to look out for time-link words in their reading. Start a class checklist of these useful words.

SESSION ②

FOCUS

● **How do you write a postcard?**

RESOURCES

● Essential Non-fiction Anthology pages 40–41 *Brochure for Uplands Farm*
● Non-fiction Skills Big Book pages 36–37 *Postcard and writing frame*
● Resource Sheet 2 *Writing Frame for Postcard*
● Tourist Information brochures and postcards (optional)

SHARED READING AND WRITING

? Limbering up Hand out some brochures to groups of children. Ask them what is featured, and how the authors have made the brochures look attractive. *(optional)*

Explain to the class that they are going to look at a brochure for a farm holiday in the Anthology (pp.40–41). Read the brochure out loud to the children.

◁) Listening focus Which words persuade you to visit the farm and which details make it sound attractive?

Read the children the postcard in the Big Book, p.36. Ask them what Sam liked best. Point out the features of postcard writing (e.g. casual tone, brief language). Look at the way the address is laid out. Draw out the purpose and audience for this type of writing. Share any postcards children have brought in.

Complete the blank postcard frame on Big Book p.37, as if writing to a friend from Uplands Farm.

INDEPENDENT WRITING

Give the children RS2. This is a frame for a holiday postcard from Uplands Farm.

↪ Extension Challenge more confident writers to write a series of three postcards charting the highs and lows of the holiday.

GUIDED WRITING — SUPPORT

Orally rehearse the language of the postcards. Write any key words and discuss the spellings. Encourage the group to write their own message. Scribe the addresses for the group.

PLENARY

Show the children the text message on p.36 of the Big Book. Talk about why these messages are abbreviated. Brainstorm other abbreviations or emoticons (*smiley face, etc*).

Tell them to work with a partner to devise a one-line text message. Ask individual children to write their message on the board. Can the rest of the class read it or suggest any further abbreviations?

GUIDED WRITING — SUPPORT

Help the group to devise an oral recount of the farm visit. Ensure they use the text and language features of a recount. Scribe their version, drawing attention to the features, particularly their use of a range of temporal connectives.

PLENARY

Discuss the recounts that the children have written. Were they able to use a range of connectives? Did they include additional events? Share the scribed recount. Identify specific text features and temporal connectives, and add any new ones to the class list. Talk about the audience and purpose of this type of writing.

SESSION ③

 FOCUS

- **What are the typical features of a recount?**

RESOURCES

- Essential Non-fiction Anthology page 36 *Recount letter*
- Resource Sheet 3 *Features of a Recount Letter*

SHARED READING

Read the recount letter to the class. Talk about the farm visit. Would they have liked to visit the farm? Which part sounds the most exciting?

Explain to the children that the letter is a recount because it has a particular purpose, structure and language features. (See RS3 for details). Compare the purpose and audience with the postcard that you read in the last session. Draw out the idea of a slightly more formal tone, shown by the use of complete sentences, events presented in chronological order, etc.

SENTENCE WORK

Display a selection of temporal connectives written on word cards (*e.g. first of all, then, next, after that, a little later, at lunchtime, in the afternoon, at the end of the day*). Challenge individual children to recount an event from the farm trip as though they had gone themselves. They must start each sentence or event with one of the temporal connectives from the board so that it links with the previous one.

(Links with GfW Unit 18.)

INDEPENDENT WRITING

Ask the children to write their own recount of the trip using a series of temporal connectives to begin each sentence or paragraph, based on the oral work from the shared session.

- **Extension** Challenge children to add more detail to their recount to give a more personal perspective on the day.

SESSION ④

FOCUS

- **What must you remember when writing a recount?**

RESOURCES

- Essential Non-fiction Anthology page 36 *Recount letter*
- Resource Sheet 3 *Features of a Recount Letter*
- Make cards of temporal connectives like: *Later, soon after, next day, yesterday, finally.*

SHARED WRITING

Demonstration writing Write a brief recount of what you did on Saturday morning, incorporating the features listed on RS3.

- **Time out for thinking** Tell the children to work with a partner and list the linking words and phrases related to time in your recount. Refer to the class list started in Session 1 and the recount letter in the Anthology, and add any further examples from today's session.

Planning for writing Explain to the children that they are going to write their own recount of how they spent Saturday morning. Collect ideas to include in a letter for them. Give them time to share ideas in pairs and to make brief notes to help organise their work.

WORD WORK

Choose a selection of the linking words and phrases related to time from the class list and discuss their spelling. Remind the children of different strategies for learning spellings (*e.g. Look, Say, Cover, Write, Check; syllables; mnemonics*). Tell them to test one another on five of the words.

INDEPENDENT WRITING

Ask the children to write their recount.

- **Support** provide the children with a selection of temporal connectives on cards to help them organise their ideas into chronological order and to use as sentence starters.

PLENARY

Tell the children to swap their recount with a partner. The partner should underline three examples of temporal connectives and check if they have been spelled correctly. Invite partners to volunteer what they consider to be the most successful sentence in their partner's work. Tell them to read these aloud to the class.

Play 'And then'. Ask individual children to tell the story of a TV programme without using the words 'and then'. If they do so, someone else has to take over.

(Links with GfW Unit 18.)

SESSION 5

FOCUS

- **What is a letter of enquiry?**

RESOURCES

- Non-fiction Skills Big Book pages 40–41 *Letter of Enquiry*
- Essential Non-fiction Anthology pages 40–41 *Brochure for Uplands Farm*
- Resource Sheet 4 *Reply to Letter of Enquiry*

SHARED READING AND WRITING

Set the scene for the children by telling them that a lady has booked a week's holiday in Barn Cottage on Uplands Farm. Now she has some further queries about the cottage. Read her letter in the Big Book. Remind the children that Mrs Brown has not met Mrs Giles and that their communication is formal. Write Mrs Brown's questions on the board. Refer quickly to the brochure on pp.40–41 in the Anthology to get some clues as to Mrs Giles' reply.

Explain to the children that this letter is more formal than the postcard they read in Session 2 or the recount letter (Session 3). Using the acetate sheet, mark the features of the formal letter (*full address of sender, semi-formal greeting, tone of polite enquiry, formal signing off.*)

Demonstration writing Using the frame on Big Book p.39, model writing the answer to the letter of enquiry discussing the style and formal tone as you write.

Planning for writing Ask the children to imagine that they are going to stay in the Farmhouse itself. Tell them to work with a partner to think of two questions to ask Mrs Giles about the accommodation, based on what's in the brochure. Share the questions that the children suggest and select two to write up, using a tone of polite enquiry. Ask the children to consider how Mrs Giles would reply and to rehearse this orally.

INDEPENDENT WRITING

Give each child a copy of RS4. This is a frame for them to reply to the questions they have raised about the Farmhouse. Remind them about the formality of tone that is suitable for this kind of letter.

GUIDED WRITING — EXTENSION

Talk to the group about the layout of the letter replying to the questions that have been raised. Challenge them to compose the complete letter, rather than using the writing frame. Monitor their understanding of layout and formality of tone, supporting as necessary.

PLENARY

Review the different types of letters that the children have encountered so far in the unit and, together, sum up some of the features of each.

SESSION 6

FOCUS

- **What is a letter of explanation?**

RESOURCES

- Non-fiction Skills Big Book p.40 *Formal Letter*
- Resource Sheet 5 *Fill in the Gaps!*

SHARED READING

Ask the children to recall the examples of letters they have read so far in the unit (postcards, text messages, recount letter and letter of enquiry). Explain that they are now going to look at a formal letter.

Tell the children that farmers are responsible for maintaining their hedges. Farmer Giles has received a letter from the local Council reminding him about this duty.

Time out for thinking Ask the children what was the difference between the recount letter and the letter of enquiry (*the first was informal and the second was formal*). Tell them that this is an even more formal style of letter.

Read the letter on Big Book p.40.

Listening focus Tell the children to listen out for examples of formal language in the letter.

Discuss the content of the letter and check that children understand it. Ask them to identify words and phrases that indicate formality – highlight these using the acetate sheet.

Ask the children to help you to identify the main point of each paragraph. Write these on the acetate sheet next to the relevant paragraph, i.e. Paragraph 1: *remind him of his responsibilities*; Paragraph 2: *hedges must be cut back*; Paragraph 3: *tops of hedges must be untrimmed*; Paragraph 4: *to discuss the letter contact the sender.*

SENTENCE WORK

Explain to the children that readers can often guess at the meaning of a word from its place in a sentence. Underline the word 'responsibilities'. Explain that it is a noun and one clue to the fact that it is a noun is that it follows the word 'your' so the reader knows that the next word is likely to be 'a something' and that is a noun. Ask the children to work out the meaning from the sentence and make suggestions.

Do the same with the words 'required' (verb) and 'adjacent' (adjective).

INDEPENDENT WRITING

Give each child a copy of RS5. This is a copy of the formal letter with some words deleted. Ask the children to work with a partner and to fill in the blanks.

GUIDED WRITING — CORE

Reread the formal letter in the Big Book. Explain that the group are going to help you to write Mr Giles's reply. Discuss what Mr Giles will say in his letter and the degree of formality that he will use. Ask individual children to write the opening statement. Share these within the group and discuss the effectiveness of the language. Keep a copy of the group's letter for use in the plenary.

PLENARY

Show the class the Big Book and compare their answers. Did everyone understand what the words meant?

Show the copy of the letter completed in guided work. Ask the class to note examples of formal language.

SESSION 7

FOCUS

- **What must you remember when writing a formal letter?**

STAGE 1 / TERM 3 / UNIT 5

RESOURCES

- Non-fiction Skills Big Book pages 40–41 *Formal Letter*
- Resource Sheet 6 *Formal Letter*
- Resource Sheet 7 *Subjects and Verbs*
- Resource Sheet 8 *Matching Pronouns and Verbs*

SHARED WRITING

Reread the formal letter on p.40. Explain to the class that Mr Giles did not reply to the letter and so the Inspector of Highways had to send him a reminder. Tell the class that they are going to help you write it.

Discuss the layout of the letter on Big Book p.41. Talk about the addresses and the formal way of addressing Mr Giles. Summarise for the class what Mr Hargreaves wants to say (*remind Mr Giles about his responsibilities*). How can he persuade Mr Giles to comply? (*perhaps he will alert Mr Giles to the fact that the Council will trim the hedges and pass on the cost to Mr Giles*). See RS6 for a suggested letter.

 Time out for thinking Remind the children that in the previous session they helped summarise the content of each paragraph in the original letter. Ask them to work with a partner and write a summary of the 3rd paragraph on their whiteboards.

Share these summaries and write the most successful one on the acetate sheet next to paragraph 3.

SENTENCE WORK

Write the following sentence on the board and ask the children what is wrong: *We was going to the shops.*

Explain that there should always be agreement between the pronoun and the verb. This has not happened here – 'we' is plural, 'was' is singular. A plural noun needs a plural verb.

Write *was* and *were* on the board and the following sentences with gap for children to fill in. *I ___ on the bus. They ___ on the bus. He ___ on the bus. We ___ on the bus.*

Explain that the agreement between the pronoun 'you' and the verb 'to be' can be confusing. 'You' can mean one person or several people. So we write 'You were on the bus' whether we are talking about one child or the whole class.

These are the agreements of the verb 'to be' in the past tense: *I was, you were, he/she/it was* (singular) and *we were, you were, they were* (plural).

INDEPENDENT WRITING

Ask the children to complete the sentences on RS7, putting in a suitable pronoun to link with the verb.

79

Find reasons why Mr Giles did not comply with the Council regulations to go in a letter explaining his behaviour. Discuss each paragraph before the children write it. Draw attention to good examples of appropriate formal language.

PLENARY

Give out the cards (from RS8) one to each child. Tell them to find someone with a card that 'agrees' with their word (i.e a pronoun and matching verb). The two children should sit down. When everyone is sitting, choose a pair to come out to make a sentence ending with the word 'sleeping'.

SESSION 8

FOCUS

- **What are the features of a letter of complaint?**

RESOURCES

- Essential Non-fiction Anthology page 36 *Letter of complaint (e-mail)*
- Letters of complaint from a local paper (optional)

SHARED READING AND WRITING

Brainstorm why someone might write a letter of complaint. Have they ever known anyone who has done this? What was the outcome?

Share genuine letters of complaint from the local paper. What are they about?

Read the letter of complaint from Mr Giles.

Time out for discussion Work with a partner and decide what Mr Giles is complaining about. Why is he so cross? Share responses. Discuss how Mr Giles expresses his anger politely. Make a list of his grievances.

Ask the children to compare the layout of the letter with the formal letter of explanation in the Big Book. What is different? Draw attention to the fact that it is an e-mail and so it is presented differently.

Teacher scribing Tell the children to imagine that they are members of the local ramblers group who write an e-mail to defend themselves against Mr Giles' complaints. Ask the children how you should start it (*Sir*). Write the e-mail using the children's suggestions, taking care to get the message across politely.

INDEPENDENT WRITING

Tell the children to work with a partner. Give each pair a sheet of A4 paper. Tell them to divide it in half lengthways and to put at the top of one column *Mr Giles' complaints* and at the top of the other column *Response from ramblers*. They should list 3 things that Mr Giles complains about and 3 responses that the ramblers make in their e-mail.

Select a text at an appropriate level, ideally one based on letters. Talk about the audience and purpose for the letters and ask the children to comment on the degree of formality. Does this vary from one letter to the next? What are the similarities and differences?

PLENARY

Role play Divide the class into two groups: farmers and ramblers. Tell them to imagine they are attending a meeting in the village hall to discuss the problems of walkers on farmland. Tell them to air their problems and then to discuss how they could improve the situation (*provide more notices, litter bins, keep dogs on lead, keep paths free of brambles, etc.*) Act as Chair yourself to allow a free and frank debate.

SESSION 9

FOCUS

- **What are the common features of formal letters?**

RESOURCES

- Essential Non-fiction Anthology pages 38–39 *Letters about the 'Best Kept Farm' competition*; pages 42–43 *Kinds of Letters*

SHARED READING

Read the letter on p.38 inviting Mr Giles to take part in the Best Kept Farm competition.

Ask the class the following questions:
Who is the letter from? What is the important message in the letter? Has the event ever been held before? What sorts of things are judged? Why might the Tourist Board want to hold such an event? Why will the farmer not know in advance when the Inspectors are coming? Why should Mr Giles enter the competition?

Time out for discussion Tell the children to work with a partner and to find three clues that this letter is a formal letter. Collect in the evidence and discuss it.

Using the acetate sheet, underline evidence that the Tourist Board hope that the event will promote the area (*Wealth of Westshire, important event, encourage more people to visit, beautiful county*).

Read the letter on p.39. Explain that this is a letter of congratulations to Mr Giles on Uplands Farm's winning the Best Kept Farm competition. Pick out the words that indicate that this is a letter of congratulations (*congratulate, outstanding achievement, holiday-makers will flock to your farm, attractiveness, make your guests welcome*).

Briefly discuss the different kinds of letter the children have encountered so far, and tell them that their independent work will be to choose their own format (*email, text, formal or informal letter, postcard*) and write to someone in it.

INDEPENDENT WRITING

Tell the children to choose two characters from page 43 of the Anthology and 'play the letter game'. Some examples of openings and endings have been provided on the facing page to help them, but they may choose not to use them if they do not suit their message.

⟳ **Extension** Discuss how Mr Giles might tell his friend in another county about his success. He might send an e-mail, a postcard or a brief letter. Tell the children to choose the format and to write an informal letter about winning the competition.

GUIDED READING — CORE

Talk about the different kinds of letters that the characters might send in the 'letter game'. Ask children to rehearse the openings and endings of their letters aloud before writing anything down. Look at the extracts from the letters, and consider whether they are formal or informal. Make use of them if appropriate.

PLENARY

Write *We are pleased to inform you* and *I am writing to complain* on the board. Tell the pairs to complete the sentences on their whiteboards. Take in their suggestions and discuss the appropriate formal language.

SESSION ⑩

🔍 FOCUS

● **What must you remember when writing a letter?**

RESOURCES

● Essential Non-fiction Anthology pages 40–41 *Brochure for Uplands Farm*

SHARED READING AND WRITING

Reread the brochure about Uplands Farm in the Essential Non-fiction Anthology. Tell the children to imagine that they have been holidaying on Uplands Farm and now they are entering a competition for 'The Best Letter about a Holiday' organised by the Westshire Tourist Information Office.

💬 **Time out for discussion** Give the children two minutes to discuss with a partner who they will be writing to, and which three events made their Farm Holiday so much fun.

Remind the children that their letter will be informal but as it is going to be judged in a competition it will need to be informative and amusing. Remember, the competition is being run by the Tourist Board, so to appeal to the judges it will need to praise lots of things about the farm.

Demonstration writing Model how to write the school address correctly laid out on the right hand corner of the page, and discuss how to sign off the letter.

EXTENDED INDEPENDENT WRITING

Ask the children to write their letters using the ideas they prepared with their partner. They can start by copying the address you modelled on the board. Encourage them to read through what they have written to check that it makes sense and is accurate.

⟳ **Extension** This group should write their letter on the word processor.

GUIDED WRITING — SUPPORT

Explain to the group that the first paragraph must contain the reason why the writer is sending the letter (*e.g. I am writing to tell you all about the fantastic holiday I had on Uplands Farm last week*). Orally rehearse each paragraph before the group writes it. Assist with spelling and punctuation as appropriate.

PLENARY

Ask the children to recall all the types of letters they have come across in the unit. Revisit the targets introduced in Session 1. What have the children learned about letter writing?

 Literacy World

INTERACTIVE CD

On the Literacy World Interactive CD for Stage 1 Non-fiction, you will find the following resources for this unit:

● Copies of all the Non-fiction Skills Big Book pages for this unit for interactive work (*Letter of Enquiry* pages 38–39 and *Formal Letter* pages 40–41)

● Interactive word and sentence work for Sessions 1, 3 and 7

● All the Resource Sheets for independent work for you to customise

● Comprehensive Teaching and Planning Guides for the unit are also available on the CD.

Linking Sentences

Read the following passage. The writer has used 'and then' too often. Underline all the examples of 'and then'. Put a full stop to show where each sentence ends.

Last Saturday morning I got up early and then I got dressed and then I went downstairs and then I had my breakfast and then I said goodbye to my mum and then I set off for school.

Now rewrite the passage leaving out the 'and then' and use some of the words from the box to link the sentences.

> **Then, after that, next, later, first**

_____

_____

_____

_____

_____

_____

Now reread the passage. Are there any more words you could leave out? Cross them out!

Name _____   Date _____

Writing Frame for Postcard

Write a postcard to a friend or relative telling them about your holiday on Uplands Farm

RESOURCE
3
SHEET

Purpose: To retell
an event

Winton Primary School
Winton
Westshire
1st June 2004
PL4 3LS

Dear Alice,

Written in
past tense

You wanted me to let you know how our Year 3 outing to
Uplands Farm went. Well, the whole day was a great success.

We travelled to the farm by coach. The journey took less than
an hour and, thankfully, none of the children was sick!

Events are
described in
time order

We were met at the farm by Mr Giles and his wife who couldn't
have been more friendly. They told us the timetable for the day
and we started off in the calving shed. The children were allowed
to hand-feed two calves with milk from a bucket.

We had all brought packed lunches and we were able to eat
them in an open barn where we sat on hay bales.

Linking
words
related to
time

In the afternoon we had a tour of the farm, riding in a trailer on
the back of the tractor. Mr Giles was very helpful pointing out all
the features of the farm and answering the children's questions.
(Jason asked how the hens laid their eggs in boxes!!) Now for some
practical advice: It is well worth insisting that all have wellingtons
to wear, as it is muddy under foot. They will need their anoraks as
well, as a lot of time is spent out in the open.

Refers to
specific
people

There is a
rounding off
statement

The children really enjoyed themselves. They have written some
wonderful recounts of their day and we have already booked
another visit for next May.

With best wishes,

Hannah (Wright)

Opening
sentence sets
the scene and
explains when,
who and where

Precise
details of
time and

Description to
help reader
picture event

Written in first
person

Reply to Letter of Enquiry

Uplands Farm
Little Wetherby
Westshire
PL18 2NN

_____

Dear _____

Thank you for your letter enquiring about our Barn Cottage.

I am pleased to tell you _____

_____

_____

_____

_____

_____

_____

_____

Fill in the Gaps!

information	discuss	sincerely	~~concerns~~	property
trimmed	required	protect	contact	users

Mr F. Giles,   Westshire D.C.,
Uplands Farm,   Highways Dept.
Little Wetherby,   Westshire
Westshire   PL1 7RD
PL18 2NN   Tel. 01777 45230

My ref: PH/Hedges   6/9/04

Dear Mr Giles,
This letter ___concerns___ your responsibilities regarding the

maintenance of your hedges.

As you will know you are _____ to keep in good order

the hedges alongside any highways adjacent to your _____.

These must be _____ back to 1m from the paved road in

order that road _____ have clear sight lines.

For your _____, the new by-law (2002) requires you to leave

the tops of the hedges untrimmed in order to _____ the

habitats of birds and insects.

If you wish to _____ any aspect of this letter please

_____ me.

Yours _____ ,

Inspector of Highways
email: phargreaves@westshire.gov.co.uk

RESOURCE
6
SHEET

On 6th September 2004 this office sent you a letter reminding you about your responsibilities regarding the trimming of your hedges.

Paragraph 1
Many formal replies open with a reference to the previous letter and summarise its contents.

Paragraph 2
Next the letter must explain why a reminder letter is needed. It must be in a very formal style.

According to our Council Inspectors your hedges have not been trimmed.
As outlined in our earlier letter, Council regulations require your hedges to be trimmed back to 1 metre from the paved road.

Paragraph 3
The third paragraph gives details of the consequences if Mr Giles does not trim his hedges.

If your hedges are not trimmed to the required width by 6th December 2004 then the Council will arrange for the hedges to be trimmed by our staff. The cost of this is very likely to be higher than if you had trimmed the hedges yourself as we will, of course, have to charge vehicle hire and labour costs.

Paragraph 4
The letter ends by asking if there are any specific reasons why the hedges have not been cut.

If there are any reasons why you have not been able to comply with the Council regulations please contact me directly to discuss the matter further.

Subjects and Verbs

Add a pronoun that agrees with the verb and then complete the sentences.

1. _____ was _____

2. _____ were _____

3. _____ is _____

4. ____ are _____

5. ____ has _____

6. ____ have _____

7. ____ go _____

8. ____ goes _____

Matching Pronouns and Verbs

I	I	I
You	You	You
He	He	He
It	It	It
She	She	She
am	am	am
was	was	was
were	were	were
is	is	is
are	are	are

STAGE 1 | TERM 3 | For use with Unit 5 Session 7: Plenary
© Harcourt Education Ltd. 2004. Copying permitted for purchasing school only. The material is not copyright free.

1 3 6 Alphabetical texts

KEY INFORMATION

TEACHING OBJECTIVES

TEXT LEVEL

T3 T17 to 'scan' indexes, directories and IT sources, etc., to locate information quickly and accurately

T3 T18 to locate books by classification in class or school libraries

T3 T21 to use IT to bring to a published form – discuss relevance of layout, font, etc., to audience

T3 T24 to make alphabetically ordered texts – use information from other subjects, own experience or derived from other information books, e.g. a book about sports

T3 T26 to summarise in writing the content of a passage or text and the main point it is making

SENTENCE LEVEL

T3 S7 to become aware of the use of commas in marking grammatical boundaries within sentences *GfW Unit 19*

WORD LEVEL

T3 W3 to read and spell correctly all the key words on List 1

T3 W14 to explore homonyms

T3 W15 to understand that some dictionaries provide further information about words, e.g. their origins, multiple meanings and that this can provide a guide to spelling

UNIT SUMMARY

RESOURCES

- **Essential Non-fiction Anthology** *Hobbies; Sea Fishing; Seamount Junior Fishing Club*

- **Non-fiction Skills Big Book** *Yellow Pages; Hobbies Dictionary; Swimming; Directory Checklist; Writing Frame*

- **Resource Sheets** 1–2

- **Literacy World Interactive** Unit 6

In this one-week unit children carry out research on their favourite hobby. They use their research to make a class book – 'Our Dictionary of Hobbies'.

5–14 GUIDELINES

Reading level B/C
- Awareness of genre
- Knowledge about language
- Reading for information

CHILDREN'S TARGETS

READING

I can find specific information in the library, in an index and in a dictionary.

WRITING

I can research and write some information and put it into the right place in a class dictionary.

SENTENCE

I can use commas to help me break a sentence into chunks when I am reading, to help me understand what the sentence means.

WORD

I understand that some dictionaries provide further information about words

SPEAKING AND LISTENING

I can listen to others and ask them questions.

Literacy World GUIDED READING LINKS

- *An Encyclopedia of Tudor Medicine* (Core)

OUTLINE PLAN

SESSION	WHOLE CLASS WORK		INDEPENDENT WORK	GUIDED GROUPS	WHOLE CLASS WORK plenary
1 Monday	**Word work** Revise alphabetical order. Discuss why some texts are ordered alphabetically **T24**	**Shared reading** Look at examples of Yellow Pages in BB. What extra information is given?	**Independent reading and writing** Give out **RS1** (replica of Yellow Pages). Group answer the questions	**Guided reading** (core) Use ICT to look up Yellow Pages and compare with brochure	What are the targets for this unit?
2 Tuesday	**Shared reading (library work)** If possible work in the school library. Talk about classification system. Set class tasks to find various books **T18** Read mini-enclopedia of hobbies in Anthology, look at index in BB		**Independent reading** Follow the library trail to find books on their hobby. Skim-read to assess usefulness **T17**	**Guided reading** (support) Discuss chosen hobbies	What hobbies are possible? Which will you choose? Why use alphabetical order?
3 Wednesday	**Shared reading** Look at language features of BB specialist dictionary entry	**Extended independent work** Research chosen hobby and make notes, using library and websites **T17 T26**		**Guided writing** (support) Help group to find information and make notes **T26**	Can you mime your hobby for others to guess, and explain why you chose it?
4 Thursday	**Shared writing and sentence work** Demo writing entry for dictionary of hobbies, using check list on BB p.46. Complete writing frame on BB p.47 **T24**	**Extended independent writing** Make rough draft of dictionary entry for chosen hobby, using **RS2** as model **T24**		**Guided writing** (support) Help group to make first draft	What is a homophone? Can you find examples?
5 Friday	**Shared writing** Return marked scripts and comment on general areas of concern **T24**	**Sentence work** Remind class about the use of commas to mark boundaries in sentences **S7**	**Independent writing** Make a fair copy for inclusion in class dictionary of hobbies **T21**	**Guided writing** (extension) Use ICT to make contents list and index for the class dictionary **T21 T24**	Did you meet your targets? How does the class book demonstrate them? What have you learned about alphabetic texts?

Abbreviation key	**GfW**	Grammar for Writing
	SpB	Spelling Bank
	RS	Resource Sheet

TEACHING NOTES

SESSION ①

FOCUS

- **Why are some books organised in alphabetical order?**

RESOURCES

- Non-fiction Skills Big Book pages 42–43 *Yellow Pages*
- Resource Sheet 1 *Pet Shops*
- Copy of Yellow Pages
- Access to Yell.com

WORD WORK

Introduce the topic and explain that the children will be looking at a variety of texts organised in alphabetical order. During the unit they will each write an entry for a class 'Dictionary of Hobbies'.

? Limbering up Think of three texts which are organised alphabetically.

Why are texts organised alphabetically? Remind the children of work done last term on dictionaries. Start off an alphabet round by saying 'a' then pointing at a child to say 'b'. Continue going round the class until the whole alphabet has been said. Repeat the activity going as quickly as you can.

Talk about different kinds of alphabetical texts: *encyclopedias* list all there is to know about things, or about an aspect of them; *dictionaries* list information in alphabetical order – usually the meaning of words, but there are other kinds of dictionary. *Directories* list information with addresses.

SHARED READING

Show the children the Yellow Pages on p.42–43 of the Big Book. Talk about the alphabetical order. Explain that some companies pay for extra space but their details are still in alphabetical order. Other companies pay for a large advert which may be positioned around the page. What extra information do you get in the boxed entries?

Ask the children where you should look for help if you had a leaking tap – under 'leaking tap'? What other words could you use? Explain that the Yellow Pages is organised in two levels of alphabetical order – the services are listed in alphabetical order (*plumbers come after playgrounds and before police*) and so are the names.

Ask the children some questions to be answered from the Big Book pages. *Why does it say 'See also'? Which shop might sell Corgi models to add to your collection? Where would you go for a transformer for a radio-controlled car?*

INDEPENDENT WORK

Give each child a copy of RS1 and ask the children to answer the questions using the information.

GUIDED READING — CORE

Work with the group to explore Yell.com on the Web. Is it arranged in the same way as the book version? Are there any features on the website that are not available in the book? Is alphabetical order useful when searching the website?

PLENARY

Talk to the children about the targets for the unit. Tell them to be thinking about a hobby to write about in the class 'Dictionary of Hobbies'. Encourage them to try to think of unusual or original ideas that will be interesting for other people to read about. They will need to have chosen by the next session.

SESSION ②

FOCUS

- **What other texts are organised in alphabetical order?**

RESOURCES

- Essential Non-fiction Anthology pages 44–45 *Hobbies*
- Non-fiction Skills Big Book page 44 *Our Dictionary of Hobbies*
- Plan beforehand a particular non-fiction title you want the children to help you to track down.

SHARED READING: LIBRARY WORK

(*If possible work in the school library for this session*). Talk about using the classification system. Explain to the children how it helps readers to find the books they want. Set the class tasks to find various books (*e.g. I want a book about swimming. What heading should I look for? (Sport)*).

Time out for discussion Tell the children the title of a book you want to find. Ask them to work with a partner and decide what category the title might come under. Could there be a sub section?

Tell the children the name of the author and ask them to find the book.

Look at the way alphabetical order is used in the library. How does this help the reader?

Look at the encyclopedias. They are organised alphabetically and have several authors. They tend to be long.

Tell the children to turn to pp.44–45 in the Anthology, to see an example of a mini-encyclopedia of unusual hobbies. Read the first entry aloud. Talk about the layout, the punctuation (in particular the use of commas), the formal tone and the illustrations. It differs from the enclyclopedia in the library in that it only has details of one subject.

Show the class the index on p.48 of Big Book and follow up a few entries to demonstrate moving from index to text.

INDEPENDENT WORK

Tell the children to follow the library trail to find books about their chosen hobby and to skim them to assess how useful they will be. Tell them to note down the Dewey number or the school reference number and the title and author for further reference.

GUIDED READING — SUPPORT

Discuss their chosen hobbies with the group. Help them to locate useful resources in the library or on the Internet and scribe the details for them.

PLENARY

Show the children p.44 of the Big Book, which has a list of hobbies in alphabetical order. Discuss some of the less familiar hobbies and ask children to say if their favourite hobby is listed. Insert new hobbies in the list. Talk about alphabetical order and second letter order. Encourage them to continue to research their hobby at home.

SESSION ③

FOCUS

- **What are the characteristics of an entry for a Dictionary of Hobbies?**

RESOURCES

- Non-fiction Skills Big Book page 28 *From a Dictionary*; page 45 *Swimming*
- Essential Non-fiction Anthology pages 46–47 *Sea Fishing*

SHARED READING

Look at Big Book page 45. This is the entry under 'Swimming' from 'Our Dictionary of Hobbies'. Compare it with the example of a traditional dictionary on page 28. What differences do the children notice? *(Both alphabetical; one just gives word definitions, the other gives more detailed information on specific topics.)*

Discuss how the information about swimming is displayed. Draw attention to the features *(headings, short description, contact information, recommendation and cost)*. Explain that the purpose is to give factual information but also to encourage people to take up the hobby. Use the acetate sheet to underline the words that entice readers to find out more about the hobby.

Tell the children you are going to read a report text about sea fishing. Then you will look at how the information is presented in a Dictionary of Hobbies.

◁) **Listening focus** What is the same in the two texts, and what is different? How is the information presented? Is the content the same each time? *(Both are upbeat and enthusiastic in style, but the dictionary entry gives club details and prices, as well as a personal recommendation).* Tell the children that Seamount Fishing Club will come under *Sea Fishing*, because that is the name of the hobby.

EXTENDED INDEPENDENT WORK

Tell the children to research information about their chosen hobby in the library. They can also search websites for further information (using a search engine if they do not already know any sites) and make notes in preparation for writing their dictionary entry in Session 4.

GUIDED READING — SUPPORT

Help the children to access the relevant information and scribe notes for them. Help them to list specific vocabulary relevant to their hobby *(e.g. Swimming: goggles, towel, etc.)*

PLENARY

Play 'Guess my hobby'. Invite individual children to come out and mime a particular action from their hobby. The rest of the class should guess the hobby and ask three questions about it *(e.g. Why did you take up that hobby? What does it cost? Have you ever been in a competition?)*

SESSION ④

FOCUS

- **What must you remember when writing an entry for a Dictionary of Hobbies?**

RESOURCES

- Non-fiction Skills Big Book pages 46–47 *Dictionary Entries – Checklist*
- Resource Sheet 2 *Dictionary Entry*

SHARED WRITING AND SENTENCE WORK

Demonstration writing Explain to the children that you are going to write an entry for the class 'Dictionary of Hobbies'. Refer to the checklist on Big Book p.46. This has some useful pointers of things to include when writing an entry for a specialist dictionary. Select a hobby of your choice and complete the writing frame (p.47), talking about your writing decisions *(e.g. the title, what information to include, how to make it sound interesting, what to tell people who want to find out more).*

Include examples of longer sentences so that you can demonstrate how to use commas both for lists and for marking off additional information.

💬 **Time out for discussion** Tell the children to think up a question they could ask you about your hobby with the help of a partner.

EXTENDED INDEPENDENT WRITING

Tell the children they are going to make a rough draft of their dictionary entry. Show them RS2 to indicate how much space they have for each section. Remind them that the first box should be a general statement about the hobby. There should be 3 bullet points of key information. The final box should give a recommendation and contact details, including a website. Leave the checklist on p.46 on display for children to refer to.

GUIDED WRITING — SUPPORT

Remind them of the notes you made in the previous session. Work through each of the sections of the dictionary entry in turn and support the children as they write their rough drafts.

PLENARY

Look again at the alphabetical list of hobbies on Big Book p.44. Ask the children to suggest names of people who might take up the hobby. The trick is to make the name give a clue to the hobby (e.g. Athletics: Mr Fitt). Talk about the differences in spelling between the hobby and the surname. Point out that this is a homophone.

Collect on the board all the hobbies that will be included in the class book. Ask the children to help you to arrange them alphabetically.

SESSION ⑤

FOCUS

- **What is the best way to present an entry in the Dictionary of Hobbies?**

RESOURCES

- Essential Non-fiction Anthology page 46 *Sea Fishing*
- Resource Sheet 2 *Dictionary Entry*

SHARED WRITING

Give the children back their marked drafts. Ensure they all understand the comments you have made. Where appropriate, direct them to use dictionaries to check spellings.

SENTENCE WORK

Remind the children of their sentence target about using commas to mark boundaries in sentences. Look at the Anthology text p.46 and ask the children to help you to identify the different uses of commas in texts (e.g. marking phrases, marking clauses, and in a list).

INDEPENDENT WRITING

Direct the children to make a fair copy of their draft onto RS2, taking particular care over spelling and punctuation.

GUIDED WRITING — EXTENSION

Ask the children who finish their work to use ICT to make an alphabetical contents page of all the hobbies listed during the plenary in Session 4. Ask all the children to line up in alphabetical order according to their hobby and check they are listed on the contents page. Make up the class book.

EXTENDED PLENARY

Ask the children the following questions about their class book: *How is it organised? Who would be interested in reading this information? What have they learned about dictionaries?*

Review the targets for the unit. Ask the children how well they think they have achieved them. Are they proud of the book they have made? If possible show the 'Dictionary of Hobbies' in an Assembly.

Literacy World

INTERACTIVE CD

On the Literacy World Interactive CD for Stage 1 Non-fiction, you will find the following resources for this unit:

- Copies of all the Non-fiction Skills Big Book pages for this unit for interactive work (*From a Dictionary* page 28, *Yellow Pages* pages 42–43, *Our Dictionary of Hobbies* page 44, *Swimming* page 45 and *Dictionary Entries – Checklist and Writing frame* pages 46–47)
- All the Resource Sheets for independent work for you to customise
- Comprehensive Teaching and Planning Guides for the unit are also available on the CD.

Pet Shops

Study the information and answer the questions.

Absolute Reptiles
Reptiles and Tortoise
Specialists
88 London Road
Worton
01487 767676

Bryant's Equine Centre
A family-run business with friendly and knowledgeable staff

Rugs and Blankets
Tack and Accessories
Hay, Straw and Feeds
Bryant's Farm, Lacey Green

01466 368709

Canine Care Plus
A wide range of accessories for your dog's every need
Open 7 days a week
Bath Road, Hemdean
01487 344765

Pet Fayre

All kinds of food for
all kinds of pets.
31 Bell Street
Kingsley
Open Monday – Saturday
01466 953762

Small Pets R Us
Food, cages and accessories for all your little furry friends

21 Market Place
Woodley
01434 667012

Pam's peacocks
Be different –
own one of these
beautiful birds
Heath End Road,
Foxley
01433 208763

Where would you go to get hamster food? _____

Where would you go to get straw for your rabbit? _____

Which shop sells food for cats? _____

Where would you go to see reptiles? _____

What can you buy for a horse? _____

What's the most unusual pet mentioned? _____

Are any shops open on Sunday? _____

What name would you give your pet shop? _____

Dictionary Entry

Literacy World